RIVKA GUBER

משואות לכיש

THE SIGNAL FIRES
OF LACHISH

MASSADAH–P.E.C. PRESS LTD. TEL AVIV — JERUSALEM

Translated by
MARGALIT BENAYA

Drawings by Abba Fenichel

First printing: March 1964
Second printing: September 1964

© by Massadah Ltd. 1964
PELI-P.E.C. PRINTING WORKS LTD., RAMAT-GAN
PRINTED IN ISRAEL

RIVKA GUBER / THE SIGNAL FIRES OF LACHISH

CONTENTS

Foreword 9

AND THY CHILDREN SHALL RETURN...

| I | Esther from Bombay 15
| II | Two Villages that Succeeded 33
| III | 'I Shall Not Die, But Live' 41
| IV | "Hada Rayis?" 47
| V | The Tent Dwellers 53
| VI | Rebellious Children 63
| VII | The Jerusalem Standard 78
| VIII | 'Go Forth' 84

THE SIGNAL FIRES OF LACHISH

| IX | The Hills of Khulieqat 95
| X | Servants of the People 101
| XI | Our First Days in Noga 112
| XII | A Change of Climate 124
| XIII | "Ana Kurdi" 136
| XIV | A "Bigamous" Wedding 150
| XV | Helping Hands 159
| XVI | 'Wisdom Hath Builded Her House' . . 170
| XVII | Jews of Abraham the Patriarch . . . 178
| XVIII | Birth Pangs of the Village Centre . . 186
| XIX | I'm a "Welfare Case" too... 192
| XX | During the Sinai Campaign 200
| XXI | Electricity for the Villages 211
| XXII | Lake Zohar 221
| XXIII | Investments in the Spirit 226
| XXIV | Who shall Teach the Teacher? . . . 238
| XXV | East and West 250
| XXVI | "Where the Outpost Used to be..." . . 261
| XXVII | The Signal Fires of Lachish 274

To Mordecai

FOREWORD

We say: homeland, native land, *but only rarely do we realize what it truly means. I once felt it very clearly, through a trivial incident. It was just after the War of Independence.*

When the battles were over and the army returned to its bases, the two villages in the south, Beer Tuvia and Kfar Warburg, were left as isolated as though they were in the heart of the desert. All the Arab villages in the neighbourhood were deserted. The road was open all the way to Eilat, but transportation was still irregular, for the liberated area was uninhabited. The "Ingathering of the Exiles" existed only in the minds of its initiators. There was no incentive for the bus company to route its buses over the highways of the south or of the Negev. In those days most of our transportation was provided by the army.

One day I travelled from Kfar Warburg to Kfar Bilu on a visit. I was delayed in returning, and at dusk I was standing on the main highway waiting for a lift. An army truck picked me up, but it went only as far as Masmiya. I got out there and waited for another lift.

And there I stood on a dark night in the middle of a large, deserted Arab village. The houses were in ruins and unoccupied. Only the windows of a single building that housed an army patrol gave out a weak light. I could not explain the feeling that overcame me. More than anything else, it was a feeling of astonishment. I thought to myself: Why, this is exactly what might have happened to us, to our settlements—we might have found ourselves in the same situation that caused the inhabitants of Masmiya to flee to some unknown somewhere, according to all the rules of logic. And we—where would we have gone, to whom would we have turned for help?

I recalled that not one of us would have dared pass through Masmiya alone in recent years, even by daylight. When I gave up hope of getting a lift, I walked towards the lighted window and went into the army post. Several soldiers were in the abandoned house, sitting and playing checkers. Their conversation was loud, and my sudden appearance startled them.

"Boys!" I said. "I've got stuck in Masmiya on my way home, and I can't get a lift out of here. So either find me a place to sleep, or take me home."

The soldiers were bewildered, and didn't know what to say. One of them was sent to ask their commander what to do, but couldn't find him, and they suggested that I wait for his return. I sat down and waited. The soldiers apparently felt ill at ease, for their conversation stopped. Finally they discussed the matter among themselves. Two of them who were supposed to go to Kibbutz Kedma the next morning decided to move the hour of departure forward and leave immediately. They gave me a seat in an open jeep and brought me to the doorstep of my home.

The wind was cold during that speedy trip on a winter night, but I felt warm. Would I have dared appeal to foreign soldiers in that way, and would foreign soldiers in a strange land have thus obeyed the commandment to honour a mother?

Long afterwards it happened that I stood once again at night in the same place, in Masmiya, which meanwhile had gained a new name, Mashmiya Shalom (Herald of Peace).

This time I stood in a crowd of settlers from the nearby villages, some of them from the only settlements founded since the establishment of the State of Israel: Kfar Achim and Bnei Re'em. They all rose in the dark of night and went out to the crossroads at Masmiya.

The state was very young. Its wounds had not yet healed, and obstacles sprang up in its path from one day to the next. The lands of the southern part of the country were still wilderness, still uninhabited, and infiltrators penetrated deep into its borders unhindered. There was also great economic distress.

At the same time, the Knesset decided that the interment of Herzl's ashes in Jerusalem was to be postponed no longer, and they arrived in the country. The procession left Tel Aviv in the middle of the night, so that it would reach Jerusalem at dawn, and the procession travelled by the longer route — by way of Masmiya — in order that it might pass through Gedera of the Biluim.

The sky was still sown with stars when I woke my little girl from her sleep. Wrapped in the morning chill, mothers with their children dozing in their arms lined the sides of the road.

The convoy arrived, and in the streaked light from the east, the ruined, deserted Arab village seemed like some marvellous court of the kingdom of Israel, to which all eyes were lifted. Hundreds of automobiles accompanied the coffin, and the procession seemed endless.

The casket was borne slowly in an open car. It was covered with a pall of white silk and nothing more. The pall itself was covered with letters embroidered in gold. The Jewish women of Vienna who survived the holocaust of Europe embroidered a thousand words from "The Jewish State" with their own hands on the pall intended for the coffin of the man who envisioned the Jewish state.

Herzl arrived in the country together with the first wave of the great immigration, and his casket was transported "on wings of eagles."

This is no legend.

R. G.

I
AND THY CHILDREN SHALL RETURN...

I

ESTHER FROM BOMBAY

How wonderful it would be to live in a world wholly good, where no man is forced to wander from place to place, where there are no problems of refugees, and where children grow up untroubled in their parents' arms. But in the real world, many are the twists of fate that may tear a man from his natural surroundings, and when this happens, he is cast upon the mercy of God and the treatment of the society into which he is cast.

Once, when I was serving in the army during the Second World War, I was on night duty in the kitchen one evening. We were waiting for a convoy of women drivers who were travelling from Alexandria to Haifa, and preparing a meal for them.

It was winter. Outside a heavy rain was pouring down. Into the large, soot-blackened hut that served as the army kitchen came a British sergeant. Drops of water streamed from her uniform. She was a sergeant in the military police who had just finished her watch. We invited her to take off her coat and get warm.

When I served her a cup of tea, I took my first look at the thin woman with the pointed nose who, like any military policeman, was not especially liked around the camp. Somehow it seemed to me that now, together with the colours which had been washed from her face by the rain, something of the severity of her glance had also vanished. I felt a pang when I looked into her eyes: in them I sensed a deep familiar, sorrow. I remarked to her that she had a hard job: on watch at all hours of the day and in all kinds of weather.

"It's not that," she said. "In other parts of the world, the winter is far harder than here. In Canada there were heavy snows this year — they haven't seen the like of it in years."

"Are you from Canada?"

"No, but my children are there, on a farm. Many of the children in England were sent to Canada during the blitz."

She took out her folder and showed me several pictures: two boys, aged about eight and five. I, too, showed her the snapshots of my three children. We began to talk to one another then, a conversation of two mothers, heart to heart.

Finally she said: "You're a lucky woman to be able to watch over your own home, and that it's unharmed, and your children are in it. London has been emptied of its children. We had to send them overseas, to wherever a Christian soul was ready to take them in and care for them."

I agreed with all my heart.

The mud of Kfar Warburg was known far and wide. In those days the roads in the village were still unpaved, and we were virtually cut off from the world during the rainy season. During the heavy rains, even the newspapers and the mail did not reach us.

But on that winter night at the beginning of December in 1949, when torrents of rain fell on the crowded camp of tents that was filled with immigrants from India, Kfar Warburg was also a sure refuge. There had been no decision in advance as to who would be sent where. The pouring rain swept everything away. Tents were blown down, possessions were drenched, tragedies occurred. The Jewish Agency sent trucks for the children, who were removed from the demoralized camp.

This was how Esther from Bombay reached me.

Actually, they had not intended to send her to me, for our house was situated in a low-lying street, across the main swamp of mud, in which a wagon hauling milk to the dairy had gotten stuck the month before. In front of the wagon — which was still stuck fast on the spot — and behind it, ominous

signs were posted: 'Keep To The Right!', 'Keep To The Left!', as though the road were mined.

During the rains the swamp isolated our house from the rest of the village. Esther and her two brothers were billeted in three neighbouring houses that stood on the only strip of paved road in Kfar Warburg.

I dragged my feet in their heavy rubber boots laboriously from one farm building to another in complete ignorance of the important visitors who had arrived in our village. That morning a wagon stopped in front of the gate. The driver was the son of one of the members of the village. Three children climbed down from the wagon, children dressed in what was then termed "winter covering", — used clothes which had been collected and distributed to the needy regardless of fit or suitability. "Winter covering" served as a distinguishing mark of the straitened circumstances of its wearers. On the feet of the three shone new rubber boots — a gift of the village, which had immediately shod the bare feet. The two larger children were dragging with them, by main force, a little girl about five years old, who was sobbing bitterly and struggling to get through the mud.

The village boy who had brought the others, a good, sensitive

lad, was very upset. He told me that the day before a truck had arrived in the pouring rain, full of children from Julis. The little girl had been billeted in his house, but they had found it impossible to calm her. His own mother was ill, and had sent a message asking me to try my luck at soothing the little prisoner.

I introduced myself quickly to the girl's two brothers while we were all still sunk in the mud. The oldest brother, Yaakov, was ten and spoke — as the children say, "small Hebrew". The second, Israel, was eight, and spoke no Hebrew at all. They had come from Bombay six months ago. At first they had been in the immigrants' camp in Beer Yaakov, afterwards in Rama, near Rechovot, and now they were in Julis. The little girl's name was Esther and she was five years old. There were another three younger children in the family. The smallest had been born just twenty days ago. Their mother was sick, and another woman came to do the laundry. I succeeded in learning all this from the eldest, who spoke a broken Hebrew and leaned heavily on the English language, which he also spoke only poorly. I picked up the stubborn little girl and took the three of them into our house.

I brought them in and left them in the house, for it was already time for the noon milking, a chore which cannot be postponed. My husband, Mordecai, had been working on the planning and organization of the first new immigrants' settlements to be established since the beginning of the mass immigration, and most of the time he was away from home. When I came back, I found the whole house upside down. The children had investigated everything in the house, scattered books and other possessions through the rooms, and had gotten the floor dirty. I told them that I had to prepare lunch for all of us and asked them to help me set the table. The boys agreed enthusiastically, and even wanted to wash the floor.

Meanwhile my daughter came home from school. Unable to go outdoors, we passed the time with a "party". We played games and made up riddles. At first glance, the children seemed happy enough, but I sensed that they were tense, and they sat there as though they were sitting on coals: a foreign land!

The eldest spoke anxiously: "It's not right! Mother, little children in a tent, and I — in a house! I want to be in tent, my mother in house!"

I thought to myself: the boy is right. It would be both more charitable and more efficient for me to take the mother in and give her a room during the rainy season and let her take care of her children herself. But that was harder to arrange than housing the children, and in all probability the mother would find adjustment even more difficult than her small daughter was finding it. Esther would not feel depressed, nor would she fear she was being a burden on me, while her mother would feel herself lonely and out of place in strange surroundings, and would be unable to adjust herself to our customs and our manners. No, the best way to help the hard-pressed mother would be to relieve her of the care of those of her children with whom she would agree to part for any length of time.

In the evening I sent the boys back to the houses of their hosts. Esther again began to cry and sob, despite my promise that in the morning her brothers would return. Nothing I could do would convince her. Unable to quiet her screams, I tried to put her to bed, but she resisted, kicking me and refusing to part with her layers of multicoloured and ill-fitting clothing. I inveigled her into getting dressed in warm pyjamas and getting into bed. Every new suggestion I made was met with a burst of fresh tears . . .

I ran over to my neighbour and brought back a large, broken doll. It was very late when Esther finally fell asleep, with the doll in her arms and myself lying beside her. But even in her sleep she sighed heavily from time to time.

In the morning she ate practically nothing, and took her stand on a chair beside the window: she was waiting for her brothers. I took pity on her and sent her to visit her brothers with the wagon that hauled the milk to the dairy. In the evening I sent for her to come back. She returned with her doll, but her mood was no better. I decided not to send her away from our house again until she got used to it and began to feel some sense of closeness to us. It would be better, I thought, to bring her brothers to her. But they came no more. I was told that both of them had rebelled, and despite all enticements had decided to return to their family in its tent. Homesickness for their mother had won out! Their hosts had been unable to bear the children's suffering, and a member of the village committee for immigrants had taken them back to the camp in Julis.

When the same member returned from taking them home, I asked him: "How did their parents greet them?"

"Don't ask! You'd have wept to see their father beating them every step of the way from the bus to their tent."

"And what did their mother say?"

"What could she say? She cried. The poverty and the filth are simply indescribable, and a tent full of children..."

To tell the truth, her mother's tears affected me far more than Esther's. I had never in all my days had her mother's bitter experience: to arrive in a new land, one that was still recovering from the shock of a bloody war, when her sole property was — six small children.

It seemed to me that the only conceivable thing to do, was to tell Esther about her brothers' flight, so that she would not cling to vain hopes. Her reaction shocked me. She wept as though her world lay in ruins: there is no greater hurt than betrayal. She had been parted by force from everything she loved and now even her brothers had deserted her...

I was upset and almost desperate: what could I do for the unhappy little girl? What ray of hope could I give her, to comfort her in her grief? And how could I understand what was in the heart of a five year old girl without even knowing her language?

I took Esther on my lap, held her tight, and said to her: "Listen to me, Esther! Really and truly, Esther! Really and truly —" I repeated the phrase several times, with all the strength of conviction at my command. "I'll take you to Julis myself! You told me your mother's name is Hirji? Hirji's unhappy, she's crying: there's water in the tent, mud, the children are cold, there's no food... Yaakov and Israel aren't good boys — Mother asked them not to come to Julis, and they went all the same. But Esther's a good girl! Esther loves her mother. Esther will wait till all the rains are finished... when it'll be warm and sunny, and you won't need lots of clothes, or rubber boots. And then I'll take Esther on the bus, and we'll go to Julis together. I'll take you back to your mother myself, really and truly!... And I'll tell your mother: See, Hirji, here's Esther! And Esther's yours — she doesn't belong to anybody else! She was just staying with me, only stopping at my house!..."

I almost burst into tears myself, and perhaps that was the secret of my success. I saw the little girl's attitude towards me was changing, and I held her tight. I kept on talking to her about her home and her family, to give her a sense of security — to make her understand that I hadn't taken her away from them, and that there was a good reason for her being with me.

Her vocabulary grew from day to day, and I discovered that I could tell what she liked or enjoyed according to one principle: if they had the same thing or not in Bombay.

Estherke is playing with the cat.

"Esther, are there cats in Bombay?"

"No."

"Not a single one?"

"No, not a single one."

"And are there dogs?"

"Yes, there's one dog."

"And what's his name?"

"Lily."

At the table we use a spoon. Esther is dissatisfied: "In Bombay" there aren't any...

"And how do people eat soup without a spoon?"

She folds her bread expertly and sucks the soup from the plate. My daughter tries to imitate her, with decided lack of success. I call a halt to the contest:

"That's what people do in Bombay, but here we do it differently. When you go to Bombay, you'll be able to tell people: 'In Kfar Warburg, they eat soup with a spoon'..."

It was two weeks before I succeeded in freeing her hair of lice and clearing up the eye infection that had glued her eyes shut in the mornings. The doctor said I might now send her to kindergarten. I introduced her to the neighbours' children, and she began to become 'naturalized'. Nevertheless, she still refused to wear nightclothes and to sleep alone in her bed. Once I asked her where she would like to sleep. She pointed to the bed, motioning crosswise, and counting the places, saying: "One, and another, and another!"

In the eyes of the little girl, it seemed foolish to scatter the few members of the family all over the house. In her house in Bombay, sleeping was undertaken in a group — a family affair, as it was in the days of our forefathers.

Esther began to enjoy many things, even from the category of "They don't have that in Bombay". She grew fond of the animals on the farm, especially of the cows, of which she was not at all afraid. At noon we would go to the barn together, and while I milked she would teach me to speak Hindustani. The difference between us was only in that I absorbed her "grammar" with the greatest difficulty, while her young mind grasped and absorbed every new word with ease.

I found that she knew far more than I had supposed. She knew both Indian and English songs, and even some Israeli songs.

"Who taught you to sing in Hebrew?"

"Shoshanna."

"And where is Shoshanna? In Julis?"

"No, Julis is so small, and that was in a place so big, like in Bombay..."

Apparently there had been a good kindergarten teacher in one of the immigrant camps, one who had taught them their first Hebrew song.

After two months in Kfar Warburg, Esther was like one of the village children, and she had many friends on our street. In kindergarten, she had, indeed, a hard time. The little ones found out how to tease her: they nicknamed her "chicken-from-India" (the Hebrew term for 'turkey'), which drove her wild with anger.

I was surprised at the fact that during all this time not one member of her family had come to visit her. Esther herself remembered her mother well, but in the course of time she grew calm and became accustomed to us. Nevertheless, we sensed her homesickness; she would collect toys and various objects in a wooden box, saying that she was going to take all this to Julis...

Once I gave her a bundle of coloured scraps and a pair of scissors. The little girl sat in her corner for hours, utterly absorbed in her occupation. Finally, from beneath her fingers issued eight dolls, all of them neatly wrapped and tied. I donated a pillow for them, and Esther lay them down one beside the other — "One, and another, and another!" — the way it was in her father's house — and covered them all with a torn kerchief of mine.

I watched her with wonder and with secret envy: she already had a complete education for motherhood, with all its virtues! I had not known how to implant in my own daughter's heart a motherly feeling save for one single doll, or at the most, two. Watch and learn from Hirji!

The children of Julis had been sent to the village in a period of emergency, until the winter was over. The Jewish Agency had asked us to keep them until Pesach. But of thirty children, not one remained except Esther. Julis is too close to Kfar Warburg, and with every visit of relatives, some child would "desert" and rejoin them.

Spring came, Pesach was approaching, and meanwhile not one of Esther's family had come to see how she was. The two of us were certain that this was not due to forgetfulness. Who knows what tragedy and suffering might have come to a family of immigrants from Bombay living in a tattered tent in the wintertime? Did they have bread to eat? Had they, perhaps, fallen ill? Had the father found a job to support the family?...

I am convinced that Esther did not forget her home for a moment. But the better she got to know us, the closer she became to us, and the more faith she had in us. Having promised to take her back to her mother, I was committed to keep my word. Therefore, she could permit herself to become interested in this life in the meanwhile. She'd have a lot to tell her mother when she went home.

When I combed my hair, Esther would remark to me: "Mother doesn't comb her hair like that, she does it like this!"

And she would put her hands on her hips and say: "My mother doesn't have broken teeth."

I made a point of showing Esther that I was deeply impressed by her mother's beauty, and she felt her superiority.

Her face filled out and her brown cheeks grew round during this time. Even in her sleep she hugged her doll; the other eight would "sleep" on their pillow at her feet.

I thought to myself: this little girl, from a family as large as a tribe, and who herself might even be the mother of a whole tribe — how pleasant would be her union with the fands of the south and the Negev, the wasteland crying for lresh young strength.

Esther was brought to the country with the first of the immigrants who arrived "on the wings of eagles", in that winter of mass immigration that flooded the land like a vast torrent. That same winter, Esther was a blessing to us and a source of comfort, a kind of object on which our spiritual welfare was dependent. The little girl from India drew our thoughts away from our day-to-day drudgery and brought a homely warmth and comfort into our house. Without her, the house would have been like a flimsy, ragged tent, unable to protect its owners from the cold and the rain.

Just before the Pesach holiday I travelled with her to Julis to take her back to her parents, but the conditions in which the family was living did not make me enthusiastic about leaving her there. Her parents immediately agreed to my suggestion that she remain with me, and were even prepared to give me another child or two. To my great surprise, Esther also agreed willingly. I told her parents that I was prepared to take the little girl and be responsible for her education until she finished grammar school. After that, she must choose for herself. She would be able to visit her family whenever she wished. I would not let her forget them, nor would I permit her to call anyone save her own parents 'Mother' or 'Father'.

During the first years she lived in Kfar Warburg, Esther made good progress in her studies and was far advanced in comparison with children of her age who lived in Kfar Hodia, the village where her parents had eventually settled. She learned to read well, to speak good Hebrew, to read music and play the recorder. She knew many poems and stories by heart, and her family sang her praises. Many times her father told us that he would never have willingly given his daughter into strange hands, nor could we have persuaded him to do so by promising to feed her and clothe her well; but he had left her with us because he thought we were good people. His opinion was deeply gratifying to us.

One day during the third year Esther was living with us, my daughter told me that while I had been out Esther's father had come and had invited us to a *brit-milah*. He had incidentally mentioned to her that they intended to return to Bombay, and he had already been granted a visa by the government of India. The father had complained of his distressed economic circumstances and said that he no longer had the patience to wait for the situation to improve...

I was startled at the information. I knew, indeed, that there were immigrants who wanted to return to their lands of origin at any price, and that we had to take into account a 'shedding' of this sort, such as there had also been with all the previous waves of immigration — but was it really possible that they would take Esther back to India?

We went to the *brit-milah,* and we took Esther with us to meet her new brother. We had a dramatic conversation with her parents, and especially with the father, who had already begun to speak Hebrew. He saw no need whatsoever to make excuses for his desire to return. First of all, he claimed, there was no anti-Semitism at all in India, and there never would be.

Second, in his opinion, there his livelihood was assured, while here he had become a beggar. He was unable to build up his farm in the settlement, because his seven children were still small, and he saw no possibility of supporting them until they grew up.

He took pains not to offend us, and declared at the beginning of the conversation: "I won't take Esther with me. Esther is yours, you are her mother. She will stay with you, in Eretz-Israel."

"If you leave, take your daughter together with the rest of your children! How has your little girl sinned against you, for you to rob her of her parents and of her brothers?"

The father was perplexed by my unexpected approach to the affair ,and continued to defend his position. However, there was no need for him to do so: we saw with our own eyes the terrible poverty. Two of his children suffering from gazezet, a disease of the scalp, had been taken to the hospital in Jerusalem, and the rest were still quite young and helpless. My heart misgave me even as I preached at him, but I took courage and spoke.

"Look," I said. "You admit that you regret having come to the country, but now you are about to make a mistake you will be unable to change or correct. Your eldest son is twelve years old. You will return to India with nothing at all but your seven children, the eldest of whom is still a boy. You must know that even if you return to India, you will have a hard time in the beginning. Both here and there you are responsible for the suffering you bring upon your children. And what will you tell them there? And remember, too, that two of your children were born here, in this country, and they won't forgive you for taking them away. Esther certainly won't forgive you..."

The family did not return to India, although all the arrangements for the trip had already been made. Perhaps Esther's hand was in this, that weak, small hand.

The wanderings of this immigrant family from India did not

end with this. The family did not settle down for four years, and was ready to pull up its roots and move on at a moment's notice.

Another two years passed. One morning during the Hannukah holiday Yaakov, Esther's eldest brother, appeared at our house. He was already fourteen years old a clever, good-looking boy whose teachers in the school at Hodia sang his praises. Yaakov was also the support and advisor of his family, a kind of small father. This time he brought an astonishing piece of news: his father had decided to leave the village and move to an immigrants' transit camp, a *ma'abara* near the city, without receiving permission from the proper authorities. As he was in debt to the authorities of the village and of the Jewish Agency for a huge sum, they had denied him permission to move into a hut in the *ma'abara*. And as he had taken the law into his own hands and had broken into one of the huts — the police had been summoned and had removed him by force. The family had spent the night in the open.

I was shocked: last night frost had covered the trees and the roofs of the houses. I saw it when I rose early in the morning.

Yaakov added that the police had arrested his father, who had apparently caused a disturbance. The boy pleaded with me and asked me to help them get permission to get into the *ma'abara*.

I was glad that the girls were away from home at the time, and did not hear the nightmarish story. I promised Yaakov that I would come together with Mordecai, when he finished work.

When we arrived at the *ma'abara*, we wandered through a maze of hundreds of huts, whose inhabitants, through no fault of their own, looked like a rabble. We saw the shameful sight which is gradually disappearing from the landscape of our country: parched earth, neglected infants, a place where you hesitate in putting one foot before the other lest you step in filth. Children were peeping from every window. Boys played at flipping a coin, little girls dragged infants along. A nauseating stench...

I asked: "Who can tell me where the family is that spent last night outside?"

Several women paused and shook their heads. The question made no impression whatsoever on them. Only with great difficulty did we find Esther's family.

The entrance to the hut was barred by a plank nailed across it in place of the door that had been broken open by Esther's father. Two policemen stood guard at the entrance. Beside the hut were piled beds with rotted coverings, washtubs, soot-covered pots and pans, bundles of rags. The mother wandered back and forth carrying a three-month-old baby in her arms, with the rest of the children behind her, all of them in torn clothing, barefoot, and dirty.

The father was not on the scene, although he had been released from arrest earlier, during the morning. We sent Yaakov to look for him, and he, too, disappeared for some time. It had already grown dark, and it got colder and colder. The half-naked children seemed indifferent. They crowded around their mother like chicks around a setting hen. The mother sat down on one of the beds and nursed her baby like one utterly indifferent to her fate.

I exchanged words with the policemen, who were also new immigrants from the eastern countries:

"Believe us, ma'am, it makes us cry too, to see them like this, but what can we do? He wants to break in by force — it's not allowed! We told them we'd give them a police car for nothing, to take them back to the village — but nothing does any good!"

When darkness fell, we saw the head of the family approaching us with energetic steps. He stopped and stood before us, tall and thin. His hair had begun to whiten during the few years he had lived in the country. He did not greet us, and we saw that he was furious.

"Please, take pity on the little ones," Mordecai appealed to him. "I've come with a pickup truck, and I'll take your family and all your things back to your home right now."

"What home?"

"Your home in the village, where you've been living on your own land for four years. Two of your children were born there, and all of them are used to the farm and the village. Your children have a school and a hot meal there. There they have a future..."

"We won't go back to the village — we'll all die here! Before, I didn't have eyes to see, and now I know all about it! I was doing the state a favour, I was working for nothing, for a pound a day. Here, in the immigrants' camp, they'll give me two days' work a week, and that's enough for me!..."

Mordecai was convinced that there was no use in prolonging the argument, and he attempted to send me back home. I refused to go. At home the girls were waiting for me to come and light Hannukah candles, while here Esther's brothers were freezing with cold, and above their heads only the stars glittered.

In the end, Mordecai appealed to the camp authorities. Even the police could harden their hearts no longer, and the boards were removed from the entrance to the hut...

Since then, seven years have passed. We attempted to settle the family anew when we ourselves moved to the Lachish area. The father promised to listen to our advice and settled for a while in the immigrant village of Noga, where he was employed as a watchman. But after a few months, he took back his promise. He prophesied evil days for the settlements of Lachish, and especially for Noga, where he had gotten to know the new settlers. — When the work of the Agency and of 'Metach' stopped, he claimed, the population of Noga would return to the *ma'abara* like one man.

His prophesy was not fulfilled: not one man of Noga's settlers returned to the transit camp. Esther's family, too, has left the sagging hut in the *ma'abara*. During the campaign to do away with these camps, the family was transferred, together with all their neighbours in the immigrants' camp, to a flat in a housing project of two-storied buildings. The father has steady work and supports his family through strenuous efforts. The number of children has already reached ten.

Meanwhile all the members of the family have grown, and some of them have already grown up and begun to take on adult responsibilities. Yaakov completed high school at Mikve Israel, and is now serving in the army. Israel will shortly complete high school at 'Eshel Hanasi', and after them comes Esther, of course, who is now sixteen and will complete her studies at 'Hadassim', an agricultural high school for girls.

Their high school studies are provided for by 'Aliyat Hanoar.' Thus the nation observes the commandment, 'The people of Israel are responsible one for the other.' And thus has a family burdened with children and with suffering produced young people who have adjusted to the life of the country, and will be capable of taking its affairs into their hands when the time comes.

II

TWO VILLAGES THAT SUCCEEDED

ONE DAY in the autumn of 1950, I encountered Pinchas, an old friend, in the bus station in Rechovot. I had first met Pinchas years ago, in the courtyard where we were living at the time, in Rechovot. The dairy branch of the experimental station which had been moved from Ben Shemen to Rechovot in 1928 was temporarily quartered in the same courtyard.

Pinchas was a dairy worker. He had moved to Rechovot when the experimental station was moved there from Ben Shemen, where he was born. He was working in Rechovot in preparation for the time when he and the other members of Kfar Bilu would found their own settlement. Meanwhile he was living in one of the huts that had been set up for the workers of the experimental station in the farm's courtyard.

The first milking took place at three in the morning, for in those days there were no refrigeration facilities, and the milk had to be at the consumer's house in Tel Aviv by six in the morning. It was Pinchas who woke us up in the middle of the night. When he went out to milk, he would dance the whole way in order to keep warm, and he would sing with all the power of his young throat. For us, this was a kind of 'midnight prayer'. He sang and danced the same way ten years later, on that deadly night in 1936 when Kfar Bilu was attacked by gangs of Arabs from both sides, and a hail of bullets filled the air and riddled every wall. Pinchas ran out to the spot designated as the point of assembly for members of the Haganah in case of emergency. When he saw that a number of the members seemed confused and alarmed, he ran forward shouting as though he were going to a dance, and the others followed him as though mesmerized.

This cheerful 'character', whose life had been filled with accomplishment and responsibility, succeeded, when his hair had already grown white, in again becoming a "shepherd", as he had been in the days of his boyhood in Ben Shemen. This time his flock was a group of new immigrants about to form a settlement near Kfar Bilu. The Agency gave Pinchas the responsibility of guiding them in their new life.

After the War of Independence, the area of Kfar Bilu was increased, with tracts of land sufficient for thirty to fifty additional farm units. Each group of new settlers set up a camp

on the tract destined to be its settlement, and the families were given temporary accommodation in tin huts. Under the guidance of their instructor, the immigrants worked energetically at building their permanent houses, striving to complete them before the rainy season arrived.

When I met Pinchas in Rechovot, his behaviour made it evident that he was in a very good mood. While we were standing in line at the ticket window, he continually exchanged jokes with a short man who was standing in front of him. In the course of the conversation, he pounded his neighbour on the back from time to time, and each time the man was carried a step backwards by the force of the blow. After the three of us had squeezed into the bus and found places to sit, Pinchas turned to me.

"This is a great day for us! We've finished the job, and today the settlers of Kfar Bilu Bet are moving into their houses. I photographed the temporary camp before we took it down, and I took pictures of the first administrative committee of the new settlement. Meet a member of the committee — Shmuelovitch!"

The member of the new committee beamed with joy. The two of them enthusiastically told me how they had persuaded the new settlers to spend the entire summer working solely on the construction of their houses, despite the fact that the wage paid them for this work was lower than what they could have obtained in town. Thanks to strict observance of this decision, they had succeeded in finishing the houses before the rains came. This was to the credit of the instructor.

Inwardly, I felt sad and envious. In Kfar Warburg, we hadn't succeeded in completing construction of the houses for the immigrants we had absorbed in our village. There were many obstacles: it had been necessary to uproot an old Arab orange grove in order to grade the land for building lots, and to drill a new well, and we had given up hope that the houses would be ready before winter came.

The women of the village called a meeting and painted a slogan on a piece of cloth that stretched from one wall of the hall to the other: "DON'T LET IT RAIN ON HALF THE VILLAGE!"

The women who had taken the initiative in calling the meeting put forward a proposal to take 36 families, all of whom had a number of children, into private houses in the village. However, this seemed to be utterly impractical. It aroused a storm of protest: How could someone take a strange family into the house? Do you think our houses are so spacious? Or that we've grown younger after twenty years of hard work?

The village was in an uproar, but the women who had made the proposal did not abandon their position. First of all, they claimed, "Rain that falls on half the village" is unnatural. In another few months, the new members will have a vote. They will never forget our behaviour if they spend the winter in a tin hut while we, their neighbours, are living in well-constructed houses. And if you look at it logically, they will move into our houses anyhow when the rains really start and they're flooded out with their children and belongings — then we'll all be running to take them in and give them shelter in our homes, like regular "Jewish bandits"! And quite probably the same members who are opposing the proposal now will be the first ones to come running — but that won't make up for our past behaviour, and to them we will still be "people of Sodom"... There would be all sorts of problems and complications in moving people into our houses in the midst of an emergency — and it would be far better to make our plans ahead of time, and to assign the new families to the members' families, according to the size of the house and the size of the family. We could also vacate certain of the farm buildings in the village and fix them up as temporary accommodation — in winter, anything will be better than a tin hut with no windows and no floor.

The debate went on for some time, but the members of the village were finally convinced of the justice of these claims. In October the new families moved to the "old" Kfar Warburg. The program was carried out at a leisurely pace and in good weather. It was an ordinary 'moving-day', with no semblance of the confused uproar of refugees seeking shelter. The program's success must be accredited to the women of the village.

I told Pinchas and Shmuelovitch about this while we were riding in the bus. Shmuelovitch protested against this "peculiar idea", and declared that he would never have agreed to invade someone's home and "get in the hair" of perfect strangers.

"Then what would you have done?"

"What does one do when there's no choice? There's not anything to do. I'd have stayed with the children in a tin hut the whole winter *'in gehachte wunden'...*"

"Well, naturally, the families living in tin huts didn't have any choice. But there was a choice for the older settlers in the village, and they're the ones who made it."

When we reached Tel Aviv we parted, shaking hands like soldiers who have served as comrades-in-arms through a heavy battle.

Winter came late that year. In November the days were bright and warm as though it were the middle of summer. An east wind blew throughout December as well, and our neighbours regretted having raised the alarm of the rains so early. But winter finally came, assailing us with a heavy assault of windstorms and downpours. On stormy nights, when it seemed as though the wind would tear even mountains apart, the members of Kfar Warburg slept the sleep of the just in their crowded houses.

At night the sound of wailing infants was again to be heard in the homes of elderly settlers. The new immigrants had come from the concentration camps, and many of the couples had lost their children. Now the families were beginning to build themselves anew.

Absorbing them was neither easy nor comfortable; but almost imperceptibly, we gained precious objectives. The people became acquainted with one another, the new settlers learned our way of life and adapted themselves to the working conditions in the village, their children began speaking Hebrew.

Every morning I saw my neighbour's daughter together with her "tenant's" son on their way to kindergarten. They held hands as they walked, and their faces expressed a warm affection. The two little ones conversed in a peculiar language of their own, a language that the neighbour's little girl thought was Yiddish, while her "tenant's" little boy thought it was Hebrew.

The age of the children of the new settlers was, as a rule, no more than three years old. Only one family had a little girl of about six, who had been born before the end of the Second World War. Once I bumped into her after dark when I was on my way home. She was late going home. I took her hand, and we walked on together. As we were walking, she asked me, like one perturbed and haunted by an unpleasant question:

"Why did you take Esther away from her mother and father?"

"I didn't take her away from them, they sent her to me. Last winter there were terrible rains, and even snow. The families who were living in tents with little children suffered terribly."

"But every child ought to be with his mother and father!"

"Of course! But what else could I do to help, when her parents have six little children and no clothes for them and not enough to eat, while at the same time I don't lack a thing and I have only one little girl. Esther herself chose to stay with us. I agreed to keep her in our house until she's grown, and she'll learn lots of useful things. She loves her parents, but she loves me, too, and wants to study. When she's grown, she'll also be able to help her family."

"Yes," said the little girl. "It's no good when there's nothing to eat. We didn't have anything to eat, either, when we were in Russia. That's where I was born."

"I was born in Russia, too."

"And didn't you have anything to eat, either?"

"When I was a little girl, I had plenty to eat, but later on there were times when I didn't."

By the time we reached the gate of "her house", we had become fast friends. I said goodbye and went on my way. From a distance, she called again *"Lailah tov!"* — 'Goodnight' in Hebrew — but after a moment, she ran after me and caught up with me and added, "Sleep well!" It was as though the usual Hebrew phrase wasn't expressive enough for everything she felt...

When I got home, I found all my "enlarged" family sitting around the table: my husband and my daughter, my adopted daughter Estherke, and my "tenants", a young couple who had survived the concentration camps, in addition to the elderly parents of one of them, an old couple who had come to them from Rumania, arriving in the middle of the winter, and who were also staying at our house. The couple also had a tiny little girl, a year and a half old, who sat in the place she liked best – on a footstool under the table, surrounded by the legs of the rest of us who were sitting around the table.

Before the Pesach holiday, all the new houses were ready. Their owners moved to "the extension", as we called the new section of the village. In our case, the rejoicing of the older settlers over the completed houses was undoubtedly even greater than the rejoicing of the owners of the houses.

At the celebration that was held on the day they moved into the new houses, there was dancing till daylight, and the women of the village prepared cakes the like of which had never been seen. I brought one of these cakes to the Prime Minister's office, where I was attending a meeting of the Council of Bereaved Parents, the day after the celebration. This letter, from the village committee, was attached to the cake:

> *To the Prime Minister of Israel, David Ben Gurion!*
>
> The Lord has enlarged our borders, and we have added to Kfar Warburg 36 families, survivors of the concentration camps, who have established new farms in our village. During the five winter months, we housed them in our homes, and today they are all moving into their own new houses. As we regard you as one of the prime contributors to the Ingathering of the Exiles, who bears on his shoulders a large share of the problems and of the responsibility, we decided to send you, as is the custom among Jews, your share of the "good things" from this celebration. God grant Israel more celebrations like this one!
>
> Signed, for Kfar Warburg:
> S. Garfinkel
> S. Tsofin

I gave the cake and the letter to Ben Gurion's secretary and went to the meeting of the Council of Bereaved Parents. The first chairman of the Council was the late President of our country, Yitzchak Ben Zvi. During the meeting, a waitress brought us the usual tea and cake. In addition to the standard bakery cakes, this time there was an extra slice that I recognized.

It was natural that the members of the Council paid little attention to what was on their plate. With the chairman's permission, I told them that the Prime Minister had given us his share of the "good things" that he had received from our celebration for the new settlers. Ben Zvi remarked in his deep voice: "We've received a good lesson!"...*

---

* A bilingual play on words — the Hebrew word for 'lesson' is the same as the Yiddish word for 'cake'.

III

'I SHALL NOT DIE, BUT LIVE'

MY GREETINGS to you, men of Marmaros-Szigot and your companions, of whom, in my youth, I heard much as tillers of the soil, men of piety and of works, sound in body and in spirit — and whom I loved from afar. I have now seen you in our land, treading the good earth and the wide fields of the south, and I love you doubly.

'The profit of a land in every way is a king that maketh himself servant to the field.' He who makes himself a servant to the field becomes a king of three things: morality, bread, and strength.

God grant that you and your children will not pursue any loftier ambition than that of the tilling of the soil...

Asher Barash

(from a letter to Kfar Achim, after a visit)

These were the first of the survivors of the camps who reached Israel. The country was still bleeding from the wounds of the War of Independence; there was a shortage of everything. For want of building materials they could not build houses, and the founders of the first village in the south found temporary living quarters in Qastina, in the half-ruined buildings of an abandoned British army camp.

From the first day we felt a special closeness to these sturdy Jews, most of whom had been raised as farmers in the land of their birth, in the mountains of Transylvania. They reminded me very much of the men of my native village in the plains of the Ukraine, where my forefathers had settled four generations before I was born, and had made their living from the land. These Jewish villages in the Kherson area were completely wiped out during the Second World War.

The victims of the holocaust in Europe from among the families of the settlers in Kfar Achim were too numerous to count. There were families where the mother had perished, together with four children. Many families had lost three children, as entire families and villages had been wiped out. The man who remained alive again took a wife and began building his life anew. *'I shall not die, but live'*...

There was no tale so terrible that it could not be heard from the lips of the members of Kfar Achim. One of them had fled into the forest and had hidden there, in complete solitude, for eight months, living on roots and insects. He did not know that the Americans had arrived, and so he continued to hide. When he fell into their hands he was overcome by fright, and the American soldiers were frightened in turn; he was certain that his end had come, while they were horrified at the apparition of a wild man rushing out of the forest...

At the first celebration in the village, when we rose to sing 'Hatikva' ,one of the women burst into hysterical weeping. I knew her as a quiet and cheerful woman, and I could not understand what had happened. It took us some time to calm her. Her teeth chattered, and she continued to weep: "... There was a truck hauling people to the gas chambers. It was full of men, all of them naked as the day they were born! And they sang... they sang 'Hatikva' *with all their might!* ..."

The settlers of Kfar Achim reached the country in many different ways: in ships filled with illegal immigrants, from the camps in Cyprus, by way of all the circles of hell. It was clear that they were men of faith not only because of their traditional Jewish upbringing, but because of the seeming miracles that had happened to every one of them. Could they, having remained alive after all they had passed through, deny the power of prayer?

One older woman stood out among the new settlers — the only one of them who had succeeded in bringing her three children safely to the country. The eldest child was sixteen. The children gave their parents every help. This strong family established a model farm. The mother had a habit of making excuses to justify herself — as though she were culpable by reason of her children still being alive! She would say: "I have to fear the evil eye: there are many people of our age here, but all of them except me are still young parents."

The woman told me how she had watched over her children during the years of the war. They had been a family of farmers, the only Jewish family in a Transylvanian village. When the Second World War broke out, her husband had been sent to do forced labour in Russia, and the woman remained alone on the farm with her three small children. The village priest was one of the followers of the anti-Semitic Kousa, and he incited the peasants to loot Jewish property. When they robbed the woman of her cows, her chickens, and the farm equipment, she took her three children and took a stand together with them on the steps leading to the village church, on a Sunday.

When the priest arrived, she addressed him: "You've taken both the head of the family and our means of livelihood away from us — take the children as well, for I can't support them any longer!"

The priest answered her scornfully: "Do you actually think that I have any interest in how you support them?"

"If not," she said, "then how do you lead your flock? Is that the teaching of your religion and your faith?"

The villagers were impressed by her words. They returned one cow and a few chickens and told her: "We're making you a present of this, only because we saw with our own eyes that you do the work yourself, like one of us."

This clever, hard-working woman succeeded in protecting her children throughout the war, and in bringing them safely to Israel. But here, in the homeland, she did not succeed in keeping all three...

The eldest, Benyamin, had already been assigned a house and farm for himself, and his parents waited impatiently for him to return from his army service. But as he was assigned responsible duties in the army, he enlisted for another two years. Every cent he earned was devoted to building up the farm.

During Benyamin's last visit home, I heard a serious discussion between him and his mother:

"Why should you do more than other people?" she complained.

"I learned from you," he replied.

"But the time has come for you to think of yourself!"

"Mother," he said. "For every one of us, there are forty Arabs, and their leaders keep them stirred up against us, and they don't want to accept the fact of our existence. So how can I think only of myself at a time like this?..."

'I SHALL NOT DIE, BUT LIVE'

He was killed by a mine near the Gaza strip.* Kfar Achim, whose members had known so much loss and bereavement, made another sacrifice — the eldest son of the village.

When we reached the silent village after dark and opened the gate of the well-kept farmyard, the father embraced us and said: "'We, too, must taste of the bitter draught, our turn has come...'"

Inside the house, the mother sobbed the melody of the traditional lament, but with unfamiliar words: "How dear you are, my country! Every foot of your soil is drenched with my son's blood..."

The members of Kfar Achim,** who left behind them un-numbered dead in a foreign land — whole communities that were obliterated — named their village after two brothers who were "sabras". The new settlers took this decision themselves. They fought for their right to the name with the government authorities, and first of all with the mother of the brothers, myself. I pleaded with them, claiming that my sons' fate was one with the country's, and that it was a sin to distinguish the two from all those who fell in the War of Independence. But the members of the village stood by their decision. For several months they suffered financial distress and did not receive the usual loans, owing to their inability to sign documents with the village's legal name.

They undertook the spiritual adoption of the parents of "the brothers" and treated them with the respect due parents in a way that was truly heart-warming. This was a gift of kindness from those who had themselves been saved.

Kfar Achim has no grown children, but neither does it have the usual grandmothers and grandfathers. Thus we became a pair of collective "grandparents", belonging to everyone. To

---
* Benyamin Roth fell in 1953.
** Kfar Achim means, in Hebrew, "Village of the Brothers"

this day, when Mordecai and I arrive in Kfar Achim, we are surrounded on all sides by small children.

The first child born in the village was named after our eldest son — Ephraim. When he was still very small, about two, I once visited the village. A horde of little children surrounded me and clung to me. Every one of them was trying to capture some part of me — a finger, or the hem of my skirt, or the handle of my purse. I did not notice that the little Ephraim was also among them, trying to push through the others and reach me. When he was unable to make any progress, he ran in front of me, raised his eyes to my face entreatingly and lisped: "I'm Ephraim!..."

IV

"HADA RAYIS?"

SEVEN YEARS after Kiryat Malachi (formerly the *ma'abara* of Qastina), came into being in 1951, a self-governing municipal council was established. Kiryat Malachi in 1958 was already a 'development-town' with a population of six thousand. When we went to celebrate the establishment of the Municipal Council with them, we rode over paved, lighted streets. We had to force our way through the celebrating crowd to reach the hall where the ceremony was being held.

In the beginning, back in 1951, it was a different story. The Beer-Tuvia Area Council, which was set up at the end of the war, began to organize settlement of the abandoned Arab villages in the area by new immigrants who came from all over the world. This was during the flood of the first mass immigration, and the Immigration Department was unable to cope with all the immigrants. Simultaneously, they began closing the 'reception camps' for new immigrants, and transferring their occupants to immigrants' transit camps — '*ma'abarot*' — in areas where work was available. Mordecai, who was then chairman of the Beer Tuvia Area Council, initiated the establishment of a *ma'abara* in the centre of our area, on the main highway, adjoining the old British army camp in Qastina.

The settlers in the older villages had many doubts about the project: Was it logical to bring a hundred immigrant families (as was first proposed) into purely agricultural surroundings, where there was no industry? How would they earn a living? What would they do in the winter, when no field-work was available?

But the pressure of immigration continued, and the camp became an accomplished fact. The grounds of the former British army camp were cleared, and not one hundred, but three hundred tents were set up and filled overnight with families of immigrants from Iraq and Yemen, Poland and Hungary, Tunis and Iran and many other countries. Almost all of them arrived at the same time.

On the Sabbath, our children would go for walks in the new *ma'abara,* to look at the immigrants from the Eastern countries in their tarbushes and long robes, and their wives in colourful gowns with wide, loose sleeves. We would go to watch the wedding processions and the Kurdish dances that sometimes went on for days, to the notes of a strange, monotonous melody.

When the rains came, the problems began, as we might well have expected. The soil of our region is heavy, and it is practically impossible to do field work during the winter. The officials of the Employment Office worked night and day making calculations and trying to attract government projects so that employment might somehow be supplied for the occupants of the *ma'abara*. The tents were not well-secured, and a strong wind would send them flying. As a rule, their tenants would not lift a finger to raise the tent and set it up again. They acted on the principle: 'The worse things are, the better they will be'. In every catastrophe they found justification for their unceasing complaints.

The Area Council, itself only recently formed, had the *ma'abara* as its chief concern, and its members were constantly going from door to door of the various public offices seeking work for the unemployed. One day, just before the rainy season, a telegram arrived with an order to set up tents immediately for the accommodation of an additional fifty families in the *ma'abara*. No explanation accompanied the telegram, but by word of mouth it was reported that the *ma'abara* near Kfar Saba had been dismantled within twenty-four hours, and its occupants dispersed throughout the country. At the time, it had become apparent that the border of the 'Triangle' was not the most suitable spot for an Arab-speaking population who had not yet adapted themselves to the life of the country.

Mordecai was in despair: How could we overnight absorb fifty additional families into the hungry *ma'abara* of Qastina? He went to Jerusalem to "pound on the table". I remained in the *ma'abara* till evening. At the time, we took care of the children during the day and called it "school". It was impossible to organize anything like a class among a population that shifted and changed from one day to the next.

That same day my daughter had gone away on a visit; waiting for me at home was only little Esther, who had come home from kindergarten with the neighbour's little girl. Meanwhile, she was playing at the neighbour's house, impatiently waiting for me. That day was an especially hard one, and I was late getting home. I met Mordecai only when we both reached our own doorstep. It was already getting dark, and each of us immediately turned to his own tasks. Mordecai changed his clothes and ran to the barn, for it was already milking time, and I went into the kitchen with Esther to prepare supper and make up to her for my day-long absence.

It was a dark night, and a fine rain was falling. Suddenly I noticed something strange among the usual sounds of a village evening: a peculiar noise, unfamiliar, like the sound of a shouting crowd.

I listened again — it sounded very strange! I went into the hall and turned on the light outside: along the length of the path to our house from the street stood a crowd of hostile-looking men who were murmuring and shouting. The appearance of a crowd at this hour and in these circumstances boded no good. The men at the head of the crowd addressed me:

"Where's the head of the Council?"

"Who are you?" I asked, for their faces were utterly unfamiliar.

One of them answered in a rough voice: "We're Kfar Saba!", and I understood everything.

Afterwards I learned that they had appeared at the office of the Area Council, near the *ma'abara,* with a long list of demands and complaints. When they were told that the chairman of the Council had gone to Jerusalem and would return only in the evening, they staged a sit-down strike in Mordecai's office and waited for him until dark. When he did not appear, they decided to seek him at his home, and walked across the fields to Kfar Warburg.

They seemed to me like a heavy cloud, filled with thunder and lightning. I knew that at this hour the men of the village were busy milking, and their families were indoors; the street was completely empty. No one could see what was happening. Should I call a neighbour, at least as a witness, or someone who would notify whoever ought to be notified? These thoughts flashed through my mind, but they roused an inner resistance: Should this be the welcome we give in our home, to people uprooted from their native lands?...

I opened the door wide and invited them to come in. The men were taken aback, and at first, refused:

"There's no need for that... We'll get the floor dirty, mud..."

I did not give in: "But you must have come on some important business — why should you stand outside in the rain? Mud can be cleaned up! The soil of Eretz-Israel is sacred, even when it's on the floor..."

They began to crowd into the house. The room was too small to hold all of them, and a number of them remained standing in the hall. I slipped out to the barn to tell Mordecai, who was busy milking.

"The people from the *ma'abara* in Kfar Saba have arrived. And they're terribly angry..."

I went back to the house and went into the kitchen, where I saw that little Esther had anticipated me. I had taught the girls to show hospitality to anyone who came to our house. The men who had appeared so suddenly caused the little girl no fear or anxiety. On the contrary, I had the feeling that Esther felt quite comfortable among them, whether because of their Eastern accents, or because they reminded her of her own family, which was also in a similar position. In any case, little Esther showed a good deal of practical sense. She brought a basket of oranges from the kitchen, put them on the table, cut them into quarters without peeling them, and thrust them into the hands of every one of the people from the *ma'abara*.

Great was their astonishment at the sight of their little hostess, a six-year-old girl. Her dark features left no room for doubt as to her extraction: she was flesh of their flesh. What was she doing here?

Mordecai finished milking, pushed his way through the crowd, and took his customary place at the head of the table. No one paid the least attention to the short, bent, elderly man wearing a khaki cap and a tattered army overcoat, inherited from our eldest son. He asked them: "What did you want to tell me?", but he had to repeat his question several times before they understood that it was addressed to them.

One of them turned to his neighbour in astonishment: "*Hada rayis?*" ('Is that the head?') ...

And then something happened: suddenly the tension relaxed, of itself. Perhaps the atmosphere of the house helped: no palace, no drawing-room, as the inhabitants of the *ma'abara* might have imagined in their bitterness, while they sat and waited for the shirking chairman of the Council. Nor did they find here a fine lady ruling her household. All this took their minds off their own purpose. And when they finally discovered, to their great surprise, that this man, who had neither title nor pretensions to dignity, was actually the head of the Council that represented, as it were, the forces of the enemy — one young man tried to recall what they had come for, and burst out with a shout:

"We can be dangerous!"

But his shout roused no echoes in the small, crowded room ...

When the men left the house, they all stood in line to shake our hands. After they were gone, we felt ourselves impoverished and empty; for although most of their demands were completely justified, we lacked the resources to do anything for them. There had come to our house, on a rainy night, members of the downtrodden of Israel. We had refused their plea and had sent them back to their miserable tents, and they, out of the generosity of their hearts, had forgiven us.

V

THE TENT DWELLERS

THE MA'ABARA was set up in the month of January, 1951. Its problems were many: work, housing, health, and at the head of the list — education for the children.

The temporary solution, proposed by the Area Council and accepted by the older villages in the neighbourhood, would today seem like the product of a disordered imagination. It was decided to transport the children of the *ma'abara* who were of school age to nearby Beer Tuvia, and to hold classes in the afternoon. The teachers from the Beer Tuvia school volunteered to teach the children from the *ma'abara*, with no extra pay, until a local school was set up (within three months, it was estimated). This plan would have been carried out had it not been for the children themselves. The immigrant children, who did not speak Hebrew, refused to part from their parents, and would not set foot outside the camp.

Having no alternative, the Council decided to organize classes at once within the camp itself, and in the mornings, so that better results might be obtained. It was impossible to find teachers in the middle of the school year. The stream of immigration had come primarily from the Eastern countries. The number of teachers who had immigrated to Israel from those countries was disproportionately small in relation to the number of children who needed their services; and those teachers who had arrived still needed a certain amount of additional training, especially in learning the language themselves.

At that time I was working as an instructor in Khatsav, a village populated by new immigrants from Tripoli. Mordecai summoned me from there, for it was absolutely imperative to set up a school in the *ma'abara*. I had no idea how one went about doing such a thing.

To Mordecai's request were added the pleas of the supervisor of schools, Michael Peled. He claimed that 'The Lord's work must be done,' which is to say, the accepted standards required for such a responsible undertaking were modified by the needs of the hour. And this was how I leapt into the raging torrent — the problems of absorption, adjustment, and education of the children of new immigrants during the first period of the Ingathering of the Exiles, in the days of "the Third Temple". Only the spiritual hunger of the multitudes of Jewish children — the nation's future and potential strength — caused men and women who regard teaching as the highest of professions to undertake this bold project untrained.

In the begining we went through a period of "pioneering". We sat on the ground in a large tent where there was not even room to hang a blackboard. Later on, we sat on the floor in a hut where there was a blackboard hanging on the wall, but where we had no facilities for writing in notebooks. However, the machinery of the government, about which there are so many complaints, moved faster than we had expected. Within half a year, we already had furniture and textbooks. Five grades were being taught in Swedish pre-fabs supplied with textbooks and all necessary equipment.

From this first experience, I learned that physical conditions are less important than the educational atmosphere, which is created primarily by the teacher himself.

I am certain that in Israel, never was '*The Pedagogic Poem*' of the Russian Makarenko read with such thoroughness as it was during the Ingathering of the Exiles. But did Makarenko, or the great Kurchak, ever stand before a crowded classroom where children gathered from a multitude of different countries were not only ignorant of the language of instruction, but could not even speak one another's language?

After a few days, I ceased to be an object of suspicion to the children, and they began to make mischief. I tried to delve into my own memories and call up pictures of my own distant childhood: how had I been treated when I behaved as they did? As far as I could recall, I had been banished from the classroom. I gave that method a trial, but in a short time the group of banished pupils crowding around the windows was larger than the group left in the classroom. Moreover, the ones outside looked far happier! I was forced to admit to myself that my teacher, of blessed memory, knew how to keep the situation under control better than I did...

My class, which was made up of over forty children, comprised a haphazard collection of children of different ages who spoke every imaginable tongue, with the exception of Hebrew. One boy from Poland, who had passed the winter months among children from Iraq, served as a translator for me: the children spoke Arabic to him, and he would translate their words to me in Yiddish.

The children differed in their levels of education. I separated them into three study groups. The ages of the pupils varied from 12 to 15, and the oldest among them seemed to be in the most backward study group — in which there were about a dozen children who had never in their lives gone to school, and for whom there was little chance that they would long continue to study. Studies were limited to learning how to read, the fundamentals of arithmetic, and stories from the Bible. I especially recall one boy, whose name was Farouz Cohen. I gave him back his Hebrew name, Yitzchak, which he had acquired at his *brit-milah*. We did this with every Jean and Sa'id, Claude, S'bikha, and Salima. Yitzchak-Farouz went barefoot and clad in rags, was far taller than I. He was born in Iran. This community was in a minority in the class, and so he quarrelled constantly with the children from all the other communities. Every day a fresh altercation would break out between Yitzchak and the pupil with whom he shared a desk, and every day I would move him from one desk to another, until I ran out of desks.

One morning I went to his tent in order to investigate his background. I found his mother lying ill. Yitzchak had quarrelled with her and thrown a stone at her. The stone struck her in the back, and she had taken to her bed.

The father did not live with her: he had moved in with his second wife, who lived in the same *ma'abara*. The man contributed nothing towards the support of his first family. Only her eldest son, a boy of seventeen, was working, and he supported his mother and his brothers. The mother tried to persuade me not to spare my strength and to beat her son "like a dog" so that he would grow up into a well-behaved young man.

She added proudly: "He needs Torah, he needs *midrasa,* he is a Cohen, a *Cohen!*"

In the last row in the classroom sat another pupil from Iran, a girl of around fourteen, well-developed and with a faded kerchief covering her forehead. Her clipped hair testified that she had contracted *gazezet,* a disease of the scalp. For several weeks she did not say a word in class, and I noticed that during recess she did not talk to the other children. She would sit in the classroom for hours without moving and without asking for a single thing. When I chanced to remember her, I would make my way through the crowded benches, go to her, and show her how to hold a pencil. With great hesitation, she began to draw lines in her notebook. And wonder of wonders! From day to day her notebook blossomed. The girl seemed to learn by herself, and her application was limitless. When I came into the classroom, her eyes would light up with gratitude from her dim corner.

When she began to read well, her enthusiasm knew no bounds. Then she began to talk, and even to make a noise. She could not conceal her wonder when she succeeded in ensnaring from within the tangled thicket of printed marks ... a word she understood.

Once when I was standing with the children beside the dining hall at lunchtime, I noticed that the girl did not join the queue. When I asked why, she replied: "I don't eat today, I have a fast."

With the help of a translator, I learned that the girl's father was dead; according to the custom of her community, she fasted on the anniversary of his death. I visited the tent of this family, and found there a blind old mother, sitting cross-legged on the floor, in eastern fashion, and smoking a nargillah. The water in the nargillah bubbled slowly with every breath. The old woman and the daughter of her old age — the girl who was my pupil — were living with the married daughter, and this daughter, the eldest of the family, supplied their meager support.

This was not the only case of one son or daughter supporting an entire family of old people and invalids. In one of the tents lived a family of twelve from Iraq. Four of the children were in school, all bright and clever. An eye disease had taken its toll of this family: four of them were left blind in one eye, and two old women, the mother and the father's sister — were completely blind. All the rest were still suffering from diseased eyes, and were under treatment. Only the eldest son was working. I asked him if it wouldn't help for him to try and make arrangements for the two old women to be accommodated in the Village for the Blind or some other suitable institution.

He replied: "They're old, and they can't live without their family. Help them here, if you want to."

Among the members of this family who were blind in one eye was also Salima, Shulamit in Hebrew, my young and well-loved friend. Shulamit was then about twelve years old. Her diseased eye had been removed while she was still in Iraq, but the eye that remained was like a glowing coal. In the large family, Shulamit was the only child who was spoiled and coddled by everyone. She had never been sent to school in Iraq. Apparently the family had feared to send her out among other children because of her disfigurement. Here her parents sent her to school, but she was unbearable. It was enough for one of the children to offend her, even in jest, for a rain of piquant curses to be showered on him, accompanied by blows and pinches. 'Wherever they were, her brothers would hear her cries, and at once they would be at her side, protecting her like an armed camp. Even I was a little afraid of the small "witch."

The children would sit down in the dining-room at lunchtime. Shulamit would sniff at her plate and decree:

"The food's no good!"

An energetic push, and most of the plates would fly from the table onto the floor. I wore myself out trying to think up a suitable punishment for this fractious child.

Once she had a terrible outburst and caused a fight. For some reason, her brothers didn't appear, and Shulamit was left alone, facing a gang. She emerged from the fight in sad shape: scratched, her hair torn out, her dress ripped. I tried to soothe her rage, and to calm her:

"And what wrong, actually, have they done you?"

"They call me 'One-Eye'!"

I knew about this. I had repeatedly stressed to the devoted instructor of the *ma'abara* one of the most urgent matters to be taken care of was fitting Shulamit with an artificial eye. But the instructor had a whole list of urgent matters, and there were difficulties and obstacles: trips to the clinic in Beer Sheva, trips to the office of Kupat Kholim in Rechovot, getting the request for an artificial eye approved by an eye specialist, and application to "Malben". It meant travelling from one institution to another, and the instructor was already running herself ragged with taking care of all the urgent cases of illness and emergency treatment.

Once I chanced to meet an optician who fitted artificial eyes himself, as well as fitting spectacles. I decided to try and take Shulamit to him in town, in hopes of finding a solution for the painful problem. The optician told me that it would be a difficult process; no prosthesis had been fitted for the socket when the eye was removed, and meanwhile the socket had shrunk so that it would not hold an artificial eye properly.

He worked diligently for several hours: he filed and measured and filed again, but each time the artificial eye would fall from the socket. Shulamit sat speechless, her head hanging and teardrops streaming down her cheeks. The fitting was very painful, but she bit her lips and did not make a sound. Finally, when we had almost given up in despair, the optician gained his objective. The artificial eye stayed in, and the colour was a perfect match. Shulamit looked at me with an expression of indescribable suffering, but now she had two eyes! I handed her the mirror, and through the film of tears shone her happy smile.

From that time on, it was as though she had been given a new heart. She became an outstanding pupil, and she followed me like my shadow. Even after I left the *ma'abara* and no longer worked in the school, and Shulamit had already finished her studies in grammar school, she would unexpectedly appear at my side during my brief visits in Kiryat Malachi, as though she had received word of my arrival. She was the first young person in Kiryat Malachi who volunteered for duty as a librarian in the evenings, for the local library. And, indeed, she could be depended upon.

Shulamit was always the first to go wherever she could learn something new: to evening classes for the working youth, to the Bible circle, to a sewing course. Her cleverness, her industry, and her "golden fingers" made people forget her disability. She married before any of the other girls in her class, and her wedding was one of the finest and most magnificent in Kiryat Malachi.

The first school year ended on a Friday. We assembled all the children in the afternoon and held a 'Sabbath welcome' for all the classes together. The parents, all of whom were invited to the party, were excited. They had never seen anything like it: the children sang and recited in Hebrew!

When the beloved first grade teacher parted from her pupils, a wail broke out and the celebration turned into a wake. Nor could the young teacher keep back her own tears.

I stayed with my pupils to clean up the hall after the party and to lock the school building. Outside the horn of the car that had come to take me home sounded. I had to hurry home to welcome the Sabbath in my own house. The children surrounded me and began to kiss my hands, my sleeves, my back. I was bathed in a sea of affection.

Next morning at home, I heard the sound of children speaking Arabic among themselves in the yard. They were three little girls from the *ma'abara* in Qastina who had come to visit me. Their cheeks were glowing from the long walk — three kilometres — on an unfamiliar road.

"We didn't know where your village was. We walked and walked on the highway till we saw it written: Kfar Warburg."

Their progress in reading was clear: they could already read a sign. I praised them and showed them around my farm. When they rose to say goodbye, one of them said in a shy voice:

"Teacher, what will we do tomorrow?"...

VI

REBELLIOUS CHILDREN

THE TIDE OF immigration rose to new heights, and in the summer of 1951, the number of families living in the city of tents reached 800. As the majority were from the Eastern communities, large families with many children, the school was enlarged and improved. It acquired new buildings, furniture and equipment, a large enclosed yard with a system of pipelines for irrigating a garden, 1200 books in the library, and the first of their readers.

Outside of myself and one other elderly teacher — Chana Rabinovitch, who was also a member of Kfar Warburg — the teaching staff were all young. Most of them were new immigrants from various countries — Hungary, Rumania, Tunis, Iraq, and Yemen. We were all unqualified teachers, but there were good relations among the staff, and the younger teachers matched the older ones in their devotion and concern for the children. We worked without counting the hours, and the younger teachers would often "banish" me from the school.

"Here, the car's already come for you! Go on home! You've got a farm, and the girls are waiting for you. We'll get along all right without you..."

And they got along all right. On my return the next morning, I would usually find some pleasant surprise — new beds and seedlings in the garden, additional shelves in the library, which was also open in the evenings for adults and for youngsters (it contained a number of books in foreign languages). Two young teachers undertook the duties of librarian on a voluntary basis for years. We gathered the fruits of our labours nine years later. Only recently I heard an envious remark from a native-born child, one of the better pupils in the Area high school in Beer Tuvia:

"We can't compete with the children from Kiryat Malachi (the former *ma'abara* of Qastina)! What can we do? Yemenites and Iraqis have sharper minds than we do!"...

It wasn't easy in the beginning. I remember the days when we had to lure the children with prizes and rewards to cooperate with their teachers and instructors. The elderly teacher would grasp a hoe or a pick and hack at the hard earth with pioneering spirit, and the children would stand around her in a circle, looking at her as though to say: "what do *you* gain out of working like this?" Occasionally one of them would hesitantly pick up a spade — but there was always a 'smart' one to remark:
"Stupid! Working without getting paid!"

However, the good relations that existed among the staff and the mutual help given by all its members, including the camp instructor and the utility workers, made their mark; and the school became a source of pride for both the pupils and their parents. There was no difference of opinion in the *ma'abara* about the school. Concrete evidence of this was the school's lovely garden, whose cleanliness and colourful appearance gladdened the eye. In the melancholy landscape of the city of tents, the garden looked like a silken patch on the garment of a beggar. At the Festival of First Fruits, in which all the villages of the area participated, the school surprised everyone by bringing to Beer Tuvia, where the celebration was held, two wagonloads of the finest vegetables, the fruits of the children's work.

"How did you succeed in protecting the garden from that rabble? Who guarded it?"

"Nobody. The children are proud of their garden..."

But neither were the first days of that garden "set about with lilies."

In the *ma'abara* was a Yemenite family, one of the first to come from Yemen after the War of Independence. The family had already gone through a series of wanderings within the country, from one *ma'abara* to another. They came to us from a *ma'abara* in Galilee. The eldest son, Shalom, was neglected and unkempt: his clothes were ragged, his hair uncombed, his hands in his pockets — in appearance, a complete street urchin. In the course of time, he became an outstanding pupil, and was one of the first children from Kiryat Malachi to complete high school. In the beginning, however, he was an unruly, quarrelsome lad, and a bad influence on the other children.

His father was a sanitation worker — a shameful occupation in the eyes of most of the *ma'abara's* inhabitants. Even the industrious Yemenites scorned this work. One of the members of Kfar Warburg, who hired a labourer from the *ma'abara* during the days of mass unemployment, told me this story: a Yemenite labourer appeared, and the owner of the farm told him to go and clean out the manure pit. The man was deeply insulted, and complained loudly:

"I came to work at whatever you tell me to, to dig with a pitchfork or a heavy hoe. But I won't go into a manure pit! I'm a *khazan,* and I pray before the ark of the covenant..."

In all probability Shalom's father had accepted this work, which few would agree to take, only as a last desperate measure, lest he be despised by his community for not supporting his family: "Skin carrion in the market-place, rather than ask alms of others."

Once a quarrel broke out between Shalom and myself. As a result of our disagreement, the boy initiated a rebellion and urged the other pupils to pull up carrots from the school garden — the fine, large carrots that we had raised and watched over so carefully in preparation for the Festival of First Fruits. Shalom, with his ready tongue, pointed out to the children that they had worked in the garden for a whole year without pay, and in the end the teachers would give everything they had produced to the Keren Kayemet. He did not draw the line at talking; before their very eyes, he pulled up a bunch of huge carrots and went home with his spoils.

The teachers regarded this as a dangerous precedent, and decided to send for Shalom's father. The father came into the teacher's room in his work clothes, which exuded the odor characteristic of his occupation. He felt uncomfortable, and refused to sit down.

I said to him: "You have a very talented son, but we can't seem to find the right approach to him. If we knew the right way, he would be a blessing to all of us. You're his father, and your son's future is more important to you than to anyone else. A son whose education is neglected will bring tears to his parents' eyes in their old age. The boy is wild — he's a mischief-maker, and this harms his friends as well..."

At first, the man tried to defend his son by attacking me, but the other teachers came to my aid, and we succeeded in explaining the matter to him. I told him that the teachers had decided at a meeting to fine him one pound, and that the money should be sent with his son. I begged him not to beat his son, but I was not at all sure that he would acquiesce to my request. I waited in suspense to see what would happen.

My pupil did not appear. His little sister brought the pound, together with a strip of grey cardboard torn from a cigarette package, on which the boy had written, in pencil: "Take your pound, but know that you've done a great wrong..."

I immediately replied to him with a note: "My dear pupil; If you can control your feelings and talk to me calmly, come to me right away so that both of us can examine our actions together, and perhaps we will find a way to correct them."

When he came, I said to him: "Shalom, come, let's exchange places, and each try to understand the other's viewpoint, and perhaps we can come to an agreement on how each of us should behave."

In the course of a long conversation, many of our points of disagreement were straightened out. To this day I keep the piece of cardboard to remind me of the best lesson I ever received in teaching, in the spirit of the verse: "I have more understanding than all my teachers."

There were other kinds of parents, too. Five children of one family attended school, two smaller brothers were in kindergarten, and there was another infant at home. The family was classified as a "welfare case" and caused the Welfare Office considerable concern. The father was always ill or getting ill, and the mother was engaged in continual childbearing; the family's sole support came from the eldest daughter. The father was eager to open some kind of "business", but he was not granted a license for it. After a violent scene in the Welfare Office, the father burst into the school and the kindergarten like a thunderstorm, collected all his children, took them to the Welfare Office and poured kerosene over them, crying wildly:

"I'll burn them with gasoline! They'll all die."

The 'merciful' father also took his two children from my classroom. I ran after the madman, and overtook him only at the Welfare Office. A large crowd had gathered at the scene of the shocking incident. They looked on with open curiosity, and with secret encouragement.

The children were wailing with fright. I embraced them, and kerosene splashed on to me as well. I did all I could to soothe the children: "Don't be afraid, he won't burn you!"

No burning took place. After his wild cries, the father fell to the ground as though suffering from epilepsy, and went into convulsions.

I took the frightened children with me, bathed them, and put them in the teachers' room. A hot drink was brought for them from the kitchen. I recalled that the same morning I had been teaching the children that the commandment to honour their parents was the most important of all, for its reward was assured in this life: "Honour thy father and thy mother: that thy days may be long upon the land..."

One day at the beginning of the second year of the *ma'abara's* existence, I was sitting in the school in the afternoon. One of the teachers had gone to the village to bring seedlings of lettuce and beets. We hastened to plant them the same day, for we expected the first rain. We looked at the overcast skies. I made a bet with the teacher that it would rain that night. While we were still talking, the rain began to pour down on our heads. The first heavy drops sent us all scurrying to the porch of one of the huts. We stood watching the rain sink into the thirsty earth and smelling the refreshing odour of ozone. The children were jumping up and down with joy at the sight of the badly-needed rain.

The next day it was very cold. Despite the torrential rains, which had continued all the previous night and the next day as well, not a pupil was absent from school: it was worse in the tents. The children were all wet and shivering with cold. The windowpanes of the hut had been missing since summer. The roof leaked. We had lacked the necessary funds to repair it in time.

The children rubbed their reddened hands together, and each one wrapped himself in whatever he had, most of them in tattered rags. The children also found a way to warm their wet feet: from time to time they would take one foot out of its wooden clog (clogs were worn by most of them) and simply sit on it till it got warm...

As that day was a Friday, we carried on with our custom of holding a 'Sabbath Welcome'. The candles we lit were blown out by the strong wind that came through the paneless windows, but our songs rang out loudly and blended with the sound of the rain beating on the tents where more than two thousand people were huddled together. These tents — an inheritance from the British army — were in tatters and utterly unfit for use in the rainy season. It was hard to find a dry corner in one. Every inch of canvas or piece of cloth was saturated with water, and there was almost as much mud inside the tents as there was outside.

After the party, I walked through the tents together with the camp instructor, Haya Bloch. We felt absolutely helpless. To us, it seemed a greater catastrophe than a fire. You can save possessions from a fire, and get the people away, but how can you flee a flood?

Those were difficult days for the people involved in the life of the tent-dwellers. I could not sleep at night, thinking of little Yaffa. Yaffa, whose former name was Latifa, was a little girl of ten, a frail, weak little creature, skin and bones. The holiday of Simchat Torah, when the entire *ma'abara* was 'merry with wine', and in every one of the four synagogues the men were dancing and rejoicing in the Torah — that day was a black one in Yaffa's life. On the same night, her mother died in their tent while giving birth to twins, before they could summon a doctor. The tiny twins were at once placed in an infants' home in Jerusalem; another year-old infant was placed in a children's home, while the other four children, orphaned of their mother, remained in the care of Yaffa.

It is hard to describe what I saw in the tent of the bereaved family half a year later, on the day — a bitter one for that family — when the rains, so welcome to the rest of the country, finally came.

That Sabbath in 1951, when the first rains fell, all the teachers stayed in the *ma'abara,* in order to be with the tent-dwellers in their distress and poverty. In the evening I went home. When I returned to the *ma'abara* on Sunday, I was met by wet children waving their schoolbooks (which were also wet), who informed me that the school was already occupied: distressed families had broken into all the public buildings in the camp.

I went into my classroom. Opposite the door was the motto: "Go ye forth from Babylon, flee ye from the Chaldeans, with a voice of singing." The room was filled with battered possessions. A camp stove stood smoking on the floor, but no one paid any attention to it. Herzl's portrait gazed down at them from the wall, a look filled with understanding...

I wanted to say something, and I asked for someone who spoke Hebrew. A young man came forward. His dress was neglected and he was unshaven, and his eyes were reddened and burning. From the way he clenched his jaw, I felt that he was prepared to answer me in anger. I put my hand on his shoulder and told him that we would bring them dry mattresses right away. My words soothed his anger. I asked him please to ask the people to be careful of the seedlings in the garden, and to go in and out of the huts only by way of the gate. The young man had expected to hear words of a completely different kind from me, and he was taken aback. The lines of his face softened as he interpreted my words to the others, who were sitting on the floor. Their faces brightened, and they began to nod their heads:

"Don't worry, teacher, we won't touch a thing, we won't take anything!"

In front of the central buildings of the camp stood two buses, ready to transport the children to temporary homes. This project was carried out in town and country in an overnight operation that was called 'Operation Rooftree'. Hundreds of children from the ma'abarot were taken into the homes of older settlers during the rainy season. The project was carried out by officials of the Jewish Agency.

I was sad at heart: again the children were being scattered and subjected to the distress of being isolated from their families, and in this way the society we had begun to build was also being disintegrated.

Suddenly I had an idea: the nearby villages had not been asked to participate in 'Operation Rooftree' out of consideration for the settlers in the villages who did hard physical work and lived in small houses; but I was certain that the members of our village would respond if I suggested transferring my class to Kfar Warburg and distributing the children among the houses of the members. I would transfer the entire class, like a beehive, and the village would also serve as a kind of practical classroom where the children would learn the Hebrew language.

Every farm in the village would be a model class for them, and they would find a teacher in every household,

I assembled the children of my class, together with their parents, who were standing beside the buses, and received their enthusiastic approval.

The people of Kfar Warburg were less enthusiastic, and there were doubting Thomases who predicted complete failure. They claimed that the *ma'abara* was too close, and the children would run away as soon as it stopped raining. But no one closed his door to them. It had already become a tradition. The year before, the people of Kfar Warburg had taken whole families into their homes for the entire winter. Kfar Warburg and nearby Beer Tuvia had taken in many groups of children and young people: groups of youth from Teheran, Syria, Buchenwald, Cyprus. The private homes of the established village had been a kind of transit camp.

After I had assigned every pupil to a home and had given them time to get acquainted with their new surroundings, I assembled all of them in the village Youth Center, which was to serve as our classroom from now on, and I made them the following speech:

"We are going to stay here and study until our school buildings are vacated and things get back to normal. Each one of you has until tomorrow to think about it. Whoever is "fearful and fainthearted" may go home if he wants to. None of the members of our village has taken it upon himself to be a mother and father to you, and you don't need it. None of us has promised to give you anything more than a warm bed and plenty to eat. We are a group here, a class of pupils. That means that we are all responsible for one another. If one of the class behaves badly, people will blame all the children of the *ma'abara*. I am certain that all of you will be homesick, but I won't allow a single one of you to leave the village without permission, even for an hour. The people of the village don't agree to your sleeping at home over the Sabbath, and they have good reasons. But everyone will go and visit his family on the Sabbath, and on weekdays, too, if it's possible. You've all come together, and you'll all go home together. Learn to accept the situation without complaining. Try to be glad that you'll be well-protected from cold and rain, and will have the opportunity of continuing your studies without interruption — And when you go back home, be glad that you're going back to your families."

The people of the village were pleasantly surprised at the behaviour of the children from the *ma'abara*. In the course of one year the children had already learned to speak a fair amount of Hebrew. After school, the children helped their hosts with the farm work, and most of the children showed their gratitude. What especially aroused admiration was the fact that the pupils did not break discipline during the entire two months that they stayed in Kfar Warburg, and did not go to the nearby *ma'abara* without permission from their teacher. Only a few children dropped out during the first days; and not necessarily the worst pupils. One of these was Salima-Shulamit with the artificial eye. This little girl, whose soul was filled with courage and loyalty, could not endure being isolated from her family.

The class did well in its studies, owing mainly to their teacher, Yeshayahu, who later became principal of the school. He would come to the village every day from the *ma'abara*, where he lived, to give my class lessons in science and mathematics. He served as a living tie of communication between the children and their parents.

We decided to give the children music lessons — a subject of which they were completely ignorant. A teacher was found — Yaakov Canaani, pioneer in the field of musical education for immigrant children. We bought recorders for all the children who passed his tests, and he began to organise an orchestra of recorders. At an introductory lesson, we announced that although the recorders were the property of the school, each child who was learning how to play one would receive a recorder and would be responsible for its care until the end of the school year. At the same opportunity, we explained to the pupils the meaning of personal responsibility for public property.

One evening about a week after the organization of the orchestra, a group of children came to me and told me that one of them had lost a recorder. He was certain that he had left it in the classroom, but he had gotten a key, searched, and had not found it. It looked as though the recorder had been stolen.

I began investigating: Who was on clean-up duty? Two pupils came forward and said that they had cleaned the classroom after school and then locked it, as usual.

"Was anyone else besides you in the room?"

"Yes, Ephraim."

Ephraim was a very wild boy.

"Why did you allow him to stay in the classroom while you were cleaning up?" I asked. "You know you're responsible!"

"We chased him away, but he was just set on making us mad; he stood and urinated on the floor in the middle of the classroom..."

The reply astounded me. I rushed to the house where the boy was staying, accompanied by a horde of children, both from the *ma'abara* and from the village. I called Ephraim outside.

"Did you really do a thing like that in the classroom where we are guests?" I asked him.

"It's a lie, it wasn't me!" he replied impudently.

"Two others saw you!" I shouted and, in a momentary fury, slapped his face.

His reaction was utterly unexpected. The strong, thirteen-year-old lad prostrated himself at my feet and began to wail in an ear-piercing voice:

"Forgive me, teacher! I'll kiss your foot!.."

I was still unable to control myself; in revulsion, I kicked the boy with the foot he was embracing.

The incident occurred in the middle of the street in front of all my pupils, the village children, and a number of adults. No one said a word to me.

I returned to my house, and found no surcease from my distress. I opened Makarenko's book, to which I often turned for help. Again I read about the clash of the teacher with the boy Zadorov, and about Makarenko's inner thoughts after the incident: "... A terrible business, ah, the first time in your life you have struck a man..."

— But it's not the same thing! I said to myself. For I had not struck a grown youth. I had raised my hand against an immigrant child, for whose very presence here I had paid an unspeakably heavy price! Even his name, Ephraim, I was still incapable of pronouncing without a pang...

In the morning we found the recorder in the classroom: someone had broken a windowpane and had tossed the recorder inside.

I did not moralize to the children, or mention what happened the day before. They were quiet and well-behaved as they had never been before. The music teacher arrived, and I was present during his lesson. One girl astonished all of us by playing several songs we all knew, solely by ear. It was hard to believe that she could play the recorder so well only a few days after she had received the instrument. The teacher did not hide his enthusiasm, and the other children grew envious:

"She lives with Sarka, and Sarka sits with her every evening and teaches her how to play the recorder!" the children protested.

The girl replied seriously: "Sarka's a good girl, pure gold! So what?..."

At the end of the second school year, the physical education teacher held an athletic contest, where prizes were distributed to the winners. More than fifty boys and girls lined up on the playing field, which was marked with white lines. The children of Kfar Warburg 'adopted' the athletic team from the *ma'abara* and saw to it that they had suitable uniforms. The pupils lined up on the playing field responded to the teacher's whistle as though they were forged into one body. It was an astonishing scene. After the demonstration of group athletic exercises, the pupils competed in jumping, an obstacle race, and other games. At the end of the contest, the winners marched up to the head of the Area Council, who pinned ribbons on them for "outstanding performance". It turned out that the champion, the best athlete of the entire school, was none other than Ephraim! This was our mischiefmaker who had scarcely passed a single day in school without causing trouble and being banished from the classroom. At that moment he stood before us beaming all over, his face a perfect picture of unbelieving astonishment and pure pleasure.

I recalled an essay of Schofman's*, telling of a school for

---
* One of the first modern Hebrew writers

backward children in one of the suburbs. The children caused trouble to everyone who lived on the street. They would knock down fences, break into gardens, and throw stones.

"— and it happened that a heavily-laden wagon, full of cement, drawn by two gaunt, bony horses, chanced to take that street and bogged down in the mud. The wagon-driver laboured mightily to move it from the spot — he urged the horses on in a loud voice, and beat them unmercifully — all to no avail. And behold, a miracle! The unruly boys came to his aid, put their shoulders to the wagon and heaved with all their might — and got it out.

"Beware of judging these unruly children, for they may well pull far more than one wagon of ours out of the mud!"

VII

THE JERUSALEM STANDARD

A REAL SCHOOL building was built by the beginning of the third school year, and some very good Swedish pre-fabs were added as well. During the summer vacation, a committee from the Teachers' Council of the Keren Kayemet came to see me at my home in Kfar Warburg to inform me that a meeting of the Directorate had decided to award the Jerusalem standard* to the school of the Qastina *ma'abara* for outstanding achievements in Zionist education and in agriculture — the first of the schools for new immigrant children to win this award.

I hastened to the teachers in the *ma'abara*, who had remained there during the summer vacation, and to the pupils, and I infected them with my own excitement: this time we were not "accepting" charity, but were being accepted, by virtue of our own efforts and achievements, into the family of the country's educational institutions, as a member with equal rights and responsiblilities.

There were more than a few fears as to the public appearance of our children beside the children of the older settlers at the award ceremony in Jerusalem. How would they meet in public, the two groups of children so utterly different from one other, even in their outward appearance?..

About two weeks before the ceremony, a messenger from the Keren Kayemet arrived with a program of the ceremony, which included singing and dancing in which forty children were to take part. The teachers of the school in Qastina distributed the many duties among themselves. I was made responsible for the children's wardrobe.

---
* A flag of honour that is presented every year to the school outstanding in its work for the Keren Kayemet.

I did not know how the children of the older settlers would be dressed, the group from whom we were to receive the standard; but I was sure they would not appear in the multitude of loud colours so well-loved by the children of the *ma'abara*. I visited the tent of each pupil who was to participate in the ceremony, took council with the mothers, and fitted the clothes of each child. To be on the safe side, I collected the clothes, took them home, and together with two of my pupils, laundered and ironed them and packed them in suitcases.

However, our main concern was the costumes for the girls' dance. We were unable to get real costumes. Having no alternative, I made a kind of short tunic for the girls who were going to dance, out of some material of a peculiar colour (which was described to me as 'banana') that we had received from the Department of Education for the sewing classes in school. I also got blue skirts for all the girls, which I borrowed from the girls of Kfar Warburg; but when we reached Jerusalem the morning of the ceremony for a general dress rehearsal and I saw the girls from the school which was to present us with the banner — girls from one of the older settlements in the country, whose costumes had been especially made for this occasion — suddenly our 'banana cloth' seemed to me faded and tawdry. The representative of the Keren Kayemet who was responsible for the ceremony took me aside and said:

"Their clothes aren't costumes, they're 'Purim'! At least get them some plain white blouses, even the simplest kind! .."

There was very little time: the final dress rehearsal was supposed to take place at 2:30, and the ceremony was at four. I ran from one store to another, but with the little money we had, I could not find the eight blouses required for the girls to complete their costumes. This was still in the days of 'austerity', and clothing was also rationed, and the stores were as empty as our pockets...

At one o'clock the stores closed for lunch. I went back to

the other teachers who were staying with the children in the courtyard of the Jewish Agency building. I suggested that they go eat lunch with the pupils without waiting for me.

"And what about the costumes?"

"It'll be all right!" I replied confidently.

How 'all right' things would be, I did not exactly know at the moment. One thing was obvious — the ceremony might well be a complete failure if the children of the *ma'abara* looked ridiculous in their makeshift costumes.

Suddenly I recalled the celebration we had held in Kfar Warburg in 1948, in honour of the new pumping station, exactly five years ago. On that day rejoicing had flooded the village, almost as though we knew that in the same year, 1948, the dream of generations would be realized and the State of Israel would arise.

The youth of the village had put on a play. My two sons, Ephraim and Zvi, had two of the leading parts. As the member of the village in charge of cultural affairs, I was responsible for supplying everything necessary for the performance. The girls and boys, who were tense before the performance, made continual demands on me for various things that were hard to come by. Some of the most extravagant demands were made by my son Ephraim, who was playing the part of a Nazi officer who tortures a courageous partisan. He wanted a black S.S. uniform, with high boots and a row of ribbons on his chest. And where could I get these for him?

I was tired of persuasion and arguments, and I was sorry then, as I was today, that I had taken on the job of supplying the costumes. I had no intimation that the memory of that day would remain in my heart for ever, as one of the happiest days of my life.

If my sons had only known how much they had accomplished, what great changes had taken place in this country in the space of five short years! And who were the children who were about to receive, as the finest of the country's youth, the

Jerusalem standard? Could I have any doubts as to the privilege of serving them, or of my own responsibility to see to it that they looked well?

I hurried to the apartment of a friend, near the Agency building with its wide courtyard, where the ceremony was to take place. I entered the house like a whirlwind and called:

"Sonia, I'm in trouble. Give me two sheets! As soon as I get home, I'll return them."

The mistress of the house, whom I had visited only once before and who hardly knew me, was a polite, good-hearted woman. My strange request did not astonish her. She opened the wardrobe and let me take what I wanted.

I chose the two largest sheets and asked: "Is your sewing-machine working?"

"Yes, but what do you need it for?"

"I have to have eight shirts ready by two-thirty."

"What are you saying? In an hour and a half — how can you do it in time?"

"I can't, by myself. You'll help me."

I began to cut the material feverishly, keeping an eye on Sonia so that she wouldn't desert the battlefield. When he came home for lunch, I sent the master of the house to the kitchen to forage for himself. To everyone who came into the house looking for the mistress of the house, I said, with aggression born of despair:

"The lady can't move from the spot for another whole hour! I'm very sorry, sir, but I simply can't release her at the moment..."

The shirts were sewn in a primitive fashion — just two seams, and a ribbon around the neck for decoration and tying. We ironed them till they were smooth as silk. I spread the shirts over my arm like a born seamstress, kissed the startled Sonia, and without even cleaning up the scraps of material, ran to the courtyard of the Agency building.

(The good Sonia devoted herself to the project with a willing spirit, and she was very offended when I tried to return the sheets several days later).

There was great rejoicing when we handed out clean, ironed clothes straight out of the suitcases to all the children, and especially when we dressed our "dancers" in blue skirts and white shirts of a uniform design.

Now we were ready for the great occasion.

It seemed like a dream to me. Were these really children of the "backward communities" singing tremulously: "*Our feet are standing within thy gates, O Jerusalem*"?

From various corners of the roof, we heard the voices rising in response: "*Pray for the peace of Jerusalem, pray ...!*"

Delegations from all the schools of the capital, carrying their school flags, went out to meet the standard of honour, which was borne aloft. Embroidered on it in golden threads was the sun rising over the mountains. Escorting the flag as a guard of honour were two rows of little girls dressed in white and carrying palm branches. The group presenting the flag stood on the stage facing the group which was to receive the flag.

I heard afterwards from the heads of the Keren Kayemet, all older men and women who had watched this ceremony year after year, that there had never been such a beautiful ceremony. I saw tears in the eyes of those sitting around the President's table, and the children of the *ma'abara* were also deeply affected.

The excitement reached a climax when the girls from the *ma'abara* appeared in their dance. Their movements were oriental, as though they had never been taken away from the landscape of the homeland. They looked as though they had always been a part of the scene.

The two delegations of pupils stood facing each other on the stage, before hundreds of onlookers. One group — the native-born children of a flourishing, long-established settlement — presented the flag of honour to the group of children from the myriad countries and persecuted communities, all of whom had only recently arrived.

A golden-haired girl kissed the flag and parted from it: "Flag of Jerusalem, the time has come for us to part. You have been dear to us, you clothed us in honour and glory!"

The boy who received the flag — a Yemenite boy, our old acquaintance Shalom — answered her in a voice trembling with excitement: " — For the sake of the Ingathering of the Exiles, for the sake of our country, for the sake of Zion, our home..."

And above their heads — the Jerusalem standard.

VIII

'GO FORTH'

I NO LONGER had the physical strength to work both on the farm and in the school for such an extended period. The teacher Yeshayahu Rosenblum, together with his wife Leah, who had become our fast friends, moved to the *ma'abara* to live, and both have made names for themselves as teachers in the area. He was appointed principal of the Kiryat Malachi school, and I was thankful to leave the school in such capable and trustworthy hands.

I went back to "tending my garden". But the stream of immigration continued, and it was hard to go back to thinking of nothing but the farmyard and the fields — although there is nothing like farm work for comfort and peace of mind. Many older members, men and women, left their villages to go and work with the new immigrants, leaving their farms in the hands of their children. The two girls — all that remained of our "younger generation" — were still in school, and could not take our places on the farm.

Meanwhile, Mordecai was absorbed in his work with our area's new population. Within seven years, the Beer Tuvia area was filled with new settlements: twenty new immigrant villages, and a *ma'abara* with a population of 3000. In the beginning permanent names were not immediately given to all the new points of settlement. They sprang up faster than the Names Committee could find suitable names. Many of these settlements are even today still known by their odd temporary names, like the village in the Negev which was called "Kilometer 108". Whole groups of neighbouring settlements were founded and assigned a common general name; they could be told apart only by their numbers: Julis–3, Masmiya–9, Ashdod–4, Imara–5.

Taking a two-hour trip around our area by car, was like taking a trip around the world: From Qastina–1 (today Arugot), a village of Rumanian immigrants; to Qastina–2 (today Kfar Achim) where there were Hungarian and Czechoslovakian immigrants; to Julis–5 (today Hodia) populated by immigrants from India; to Ashdod–2 (Bet Ezra) a village of Iraqi immigrants; to Ashdod–3 (Imunim) one of Egyptian immigrants; to Betanya–1 (Sh'tulim) with Yemenite immigrants; to Betanya–2 (Azriqam), with Tunisian immigrants; to New Masmiya (Khatsav), with Tripolitanian immigrants; and from there to Masmiya–9 (Talmei-Yekhiel), with Bulgarian immigrants. Each village differed from the neighbours in its language, its culture, and its customs.

The wife of the President, Rachel Yanait Ben-Zvi, suggested that I join the first secretariat of Keren Bet Hanasi Leyaldei Olim (The President's Fund for Immigrant Children), founded through her initiative. The Fund's goal was the foundation and development of children's libraries in the schools of new immigrant settlements. The farm villages were settled mainly by immigrants from the Eastern communities, most of whom brought no books with them. It was a worthy goal — to encourage the children of new immigrants to acquire the habit of reading books generally by providing them with suitable libraries.

The suggested project won my heart for several reasons: the warm approach of Rachel Ben-Zvi to the project and towards the people who helped her put it into operation; my belief in the importance of furthering the cultural development of the new settlements; and, most important, the opportunity offered me of devoting to this work only what time I could really spare, at my own convenience. After years of the stringent demands made on me while I was teaching or serving as an instructor (in addition to my farm work), this for me, was an almost effortless occupation.

In all the villages I visited in the Negev, I tried to keep in touch with the teachers and the people responsible for cultural activities. Through repeated visits and exchange of letters, I would adjust the number and type of books to the anticipated requirements of the village. Even the young Beer Sheva became the concern of Keren Bet Hanasi. Every visit I made to Beer Sheva left me marvelling: the city grew before my very eyes, as though by magic.

The pioneer of education in the Negev, Aryeh Simon, supervisor of schools in the south and in the Negev, founded a seminar in Beer Sheva for completing the education of 'unqualified' teachers, who were, at the time, doing most of the teaching in the schools. Simon showed great interest in the project of libraries for the schools, and invited me to give several lectures in the seminar on the management of libraries for children of new immigrants. A day that I travelled to the Negev was a holiday for me.

If I was ever envied, it was by Rachel Ben-Zvi. She always waited eagerly for my stories about what was going on in the settlements of the Negev, and about the lives of the families living in the cement-block houses, with whom I would occasionally spend the night. She supplied me with a constant flow of gifts and sweets for the children of the Negev, among them a transistor radio — in those days an innovation that drew crowds of children around me in every village I visited. When I arrived at a school, I would produce from my heavy handbag a variety of presents to the delight of all the children. The supervisor of schools in the Negev, whom I encountered by chance as he was waiting for a lift at the crossroads of the highway, once said to me:

"I'm only surprised you don't produce a coach and pair out of that handbag."

Those two years were an education for me. I learned the geography of the northern Negev which borders the Lachish area, uninhabited in those years, dominion of desert winds and bands of infiltrators. I got to know the problems of the settlers in the new immigrant settlements from a more objective viewpoint as I myself was not an "interested party."

We have already grown accustomed to the change that has taken place in the landscape of our country with the growth of the trees planted along all the highways. Where the trees were well taken care of, and where they escaped the continual hazard of brush-fires, pleasant avenues have grown up, providing shade and refreshment. But nowhere do the trees delight the eye as they do in the barren landscape of the light-coloured, monotonous plateau of loess. Every patch of green, every fresh seedling waves above it like a conquering banner. That year acacias were planted on the 'Famine Road'. However, the first year many trees were denuded of their branches by people who needed leafy branches for the Feast of Succoth; and the second year, a heavy plague of locusts covered the area around the village of Patish and destroyed every green leaf. The guardian angel of trees needed any help he could get, and indeed we gave him as much as we were able.

This was during the period when Ben Gurion was living in S'deh Boker, and for a while it was as though the country had shifted its balance. The Negev drew people to it like some powerful lodestone. I could not pass without a tremor the memorial on the hill of Khulieqat, on the road to Beer Sheva, where our son Zvi fell in the War of Independence. Opposite this hill stands Mitsudat-Yoav, formerly the police station of Iraq-Suidan. Nearby our son Ephraim had guided the convoy that brought supplies to the kibbutzim of Gat and Gal'on, which were under siege for an entire year. Many were the mines laid for the convoys in those days, and many of the country's sons fell in that way.

"The Negev is the cradle of our nation, the weak point of the state, and its great hope.

"'When Abraham was commanded to leave his country and his kindred in Ur of the Chaldees for the Promised Land — he left and travelled to the Negev. After the famine forced him to go down into Egypt — he returned to the Negev.

"The prophets never accepted the desolation of the Negev, and Isaiah ben Amotz prophesied: "The wilderness and the parched land shall be glad; and the desert shall rejoice, and blossom as the rose."

"If the nation does not vanquish the desert, the desert may vanquish the nation."

(David Ben-Gurion, in his preface to the book
"Know the Negev", edited by M. Deshe and Y. Goren)

Where is the border of the Negev? In 1937, Bracha Habas wrote about the founding of Kfar Menachem: "Thirty people on the border of the Negev — and the spot is so far away and so isolated! Six and a half kilometres from Gedera as the crow flies." But nine years after she wrote these words, the operation of the "Eleven settlement points in the Negev" was carried out. The members of the Haganah chose the evening after the Day of Atonement in 1947 as the most suitable for camouflaging their goal. Twenty-five men from Kfar Warburg also joined them. They helped with the founding of Kelta, today Khatzerim. Our son Ephraim was filled with pride at taking part in the operation together with the older members of the village, every one of whom was hand-picked for this bold and highly secret project.

In April 1955, we offered our services to the Immigration Department of the Jewish Agency. In reply to our application, Ra'anan Weitz wrote us, in the name of the Department: "I was glad to receive your letter, in which you placed yourselves at the disposal of the authorities in charge of the project in the Lachish region. The administrative office of the Lachish region will inform you shortly about their arrangements for 'harnessing' you to the project. People like yourselves strengthen my belief and certainty in our total victory."

When news reached us of the new settlement plan for the Lachish region, our decision was easily made. True, there were eleven cows standing in our barn, but our pride and joy now was no longer the barn.

Little Esther, who loved us and had grown up in our house for six years, tipped the scales. Her family, which was constantly increasing in size, still languished in appalling poverty in their dilapidated hut in the *ma'abara*. We hoped that Esther's father had learned from his experience, and we suggested to her parents that they try their luck in the new Lachish region. Two of their sons were already grown, and their daughter Esther had been educated on a farm in an established village. We suggested that when we moved to Lachish, they take a farm in Noga, near us, for the sake of "uniting the family", and for the happiness of our shared daughter. The parents agreed willingly, and we believed them.

When we first went to Lachish, we did not think of leaving our farm completely. We handed over our house, by means of a contract signed between us and the secretariat of Kfar Warburg. The rental contract was for four years, till the first of May,

1959 — the date we expected our daughter to return from her military service, which also fitted in with the period we planned to work in Lachish. The secretariat of the village had our permission to rent our house and farm to whomever they saw fit, and the rental would cover our share of the village taxes. Our farm in Kfar Warburg had no debts whatsoever.

By chance, I was alone at home when a purchaser came for our last cow. Our neighbour Baruch, a loyal friend, helped me come to an agreement with the purchaser — a new settler in a new immigrants' village — and also helped me get the cow out to the road. I invited the purchaser to drink a toast to the success of his purchase, as is the custom among farmers. I also begged Baruch to join us.

When I served him the glass of wine, Baruch drew back and said:

"No, I won't drink with you now! When you come back to the village and your daughter Hayale begins to build up the farm again, and when we put the first cow back into the same barn — I'll reserve the right for myself to tie her up in her place. Only then will I drink with you, and we'll have a drink deserving of the name!"

Our decision to turn the farm over to the village completely was made only after a year had passed, after we had been 'naturalized' in Lachish and had become its 'old-time settlers'. It was as though we had a premonition that we would not have the strength to undergo the severe trials awaiting us here unless we burned our bridges behind us and bound our personal happiness to the success of the project in Lachish. The sum we received from the sale of our farm in Kfar Warburg was donated to the Government for defense needs. The rope followed the bucket.

When we informed our daughter, who was studying at Bet-Yerakh in the Jordan Valley, of our final decision to move to Lachish, she wrote us:

"I am frail in comparison with you, the youngest of the young, as you set out to realize this imperative goal, one which is in keeping with your strength and your spirit. And through the power of that spirit in which you now march forward hand in hand, Estherke and I will follow you. Our love and our admiration go with you on your way."

II

THE SIGNAL FIRES OF LACHISH

IX

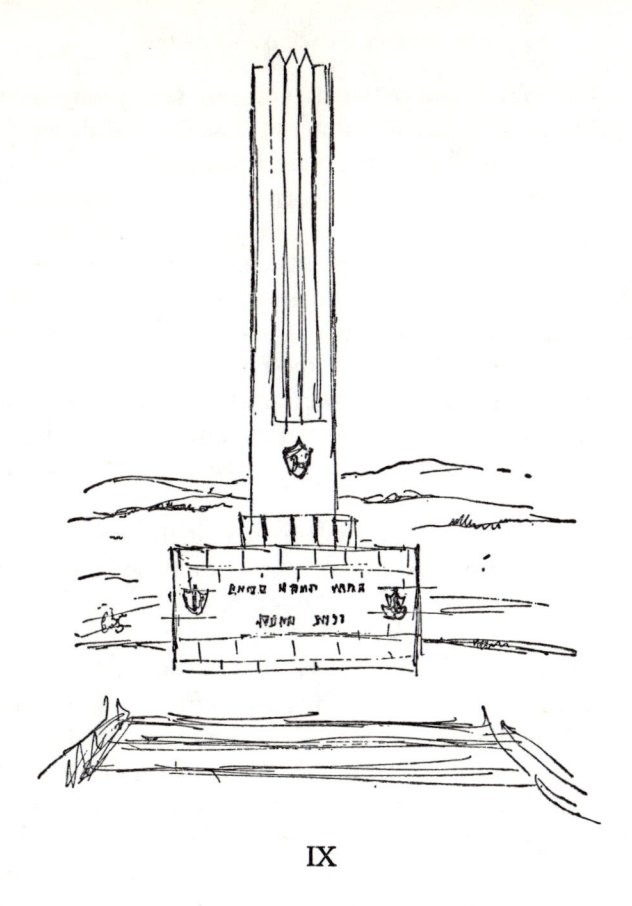

THE HILLS OF KHULIEQAT

"The landscape is really beautiful here, not like the barren waste of the Negev. There are many hills here, and a sprinkling of olive trees and a handful of carobs, and a deserted Arab village with mud huts, and vast uninhabited expanses..."

>(from the last letter of Zvi Guber,
>at the army post in Khulieqat, Hill 138)

No TRACE remains of the mud huts of the village of Khulieqat, nor of the "vast uninhabited expanses." The young settlements of Lachish spread out as far as you can see: young groves, vineyards, broad fields of cotton, oil drillings, and the artificial lake of Zohar — all these surround Khulieqat.

This hill alone has not surrendered to the plough nor to the oil drill. Has it been forgotten, or passed by? The same trees and vines planted by the Arabs of Khulieqat still sustain a little life in the limy soil, untrodden by man since the day of the War of Independence. Everything is the same as it was then, except for what the wind and the rain have nibbled away — the same long, winding communication trenches, ruined bunkers, scraps of iron, empty ammunition shells. The only thing that has been added is a marble plaque bearing the names of the fallen.

Battles were fought over every foot of the land here, and much blood was spilled in the capture of these hills. On one of them, on the road to Beer Sheva, towers a memorial with 126 names and the words:

Wayfarer, as you go down to the Negev — remember us!

When oil was first discovered in the country, a short distance from that hill, the news flashed through the country like lightning, people who wanted to see the marvel with their own eyes streamed to Khulieqat from all parts of the country — to stare at the fine spray of thick liquid and the oil drillers, covered with black and bent with fatigue after a night of vigil. One man with a small jar of oil in his hand pushed his way through to the engineer and pleaded:

"Please, write down on a piece of paper that the oil is from Khulieqat, because otherwise they won't believe me in town!"

The engineer granted his request and wrote:

"Wayfarer, as you go down to the Negev, remember us!"

The settlement of the Negev, which began at the end of the war, skipped Lachish, and the huge triangle between the Jerusalem corridor, the coastal plain, and the hills of Beer Sheva waited for six years, until the pipeline from the Yarkon river reached it. When the water started to flow, the region awakened to a new life.

The project for reviving the ancient, sleeping region was not carried out on conventional lines. Take, for example, the cotton gin — the first building to go up in Kiryat Gat. The cotton was already blossoming in the fields of Lachish, but the gin was not yet built and there was no time for orderly construction. The roof was raised in order to shelter the machines that were already installed. The gin was working in three shifts, and at the same time the walls of the plant were being built around the busy machines. Permanent housing for the workers was erected at a later stage.

In May 1955, there was as yet no gin, nor even a sign of Kiryat-Gat. We were given a hastily-sketched map which bore a dot marked with the name 'Kiryat-Gat'. When we left Kfar Warburg, we decided to go by way of the Sa'ad road. There was the ever-present danger, in those days, of encountering 'fedayin' (armed infiltrators) in any deserted area in the southern part of the country. When we left the Sa'ad road for the road that went to Bet Guvrin, we entered unknown territory. The countryside was deserted and uninhabited, and we met no vehicles at all.

We passed the Falujja crossroads and travelled for another two kilometres. According to the map, 'Kiryat-Gat' should have been on our right. We looked suspiciously at the sides of the bare hills: many of them had been mined by the Egyptians during the war. Because of the twin dangers — running onto a mine or running into infiltrators — we retraced our steps and went back to Kfar Warburg without locating the spot where the new town of Kiryat-Gat was to arise.

The first settlements in the region were called, as was usual in those days, the 'Lachishes': Lachish-1, Lachish-2, Lachish-3. Only later was every settlement given its own name. Lachish-1— the first settlement established beyond the Negba police station to the east — was named 'Otsem' (Might), in remembrance of the mighty battles which were fought on this spot.

After the bitter experience of immigrant camps and *ma'abarot*, it was decided that in the future new immigrants would be taken directly from the ship to their points of settlement. What took place, actually, was this: trucks would arrive filled with immigrants from North Africa; when they arrived at the small huts, scattered and isolated as though they were in the middle of the desert, the immigrants would protest energetically and refuse to leave the trucks. This is what happened in both Luzit and Shakhar. The efforts of the Agency workers to persuade them went on for hours, but the immigrants would not surrender:

"We have committed no crime, we have done no wrong, we will not agree to let ourselves be sent to this penal colony!"

Only when night fell did the settlers of Shakhar leave the trucks and go into the huts, broken-hearted. When we saw to it that all of them had received the food prepared for them and that beds had been distributed to every hut, we — Mordecai and I — also went "home", to Lachish-3, today Noga, which was about two kilometres away from Shakhar.

The night was dark. There were no lights showing in the area, and we could not find the dirt road that connected the two villages. In whatever direction we travelled, we encountered great clods of virgin earth, which had just been ploughed for the first time by the tractor. It was quite possible that if we went on without knowing where we were going, we might very well reach... the Gaza Strip.

That night we kept losing our way and circling the tractor station, which is still there, on the spot where the village centre of Nehora was later built. The tractors and combines stood in the open field. At first we were afraid to go near them, lest we be welcomed with a bullet by one of the watchmen. It was a baseless fear: the watchmen, who lived in Noga, chose to guard the tractor station from their respective houses, and with good reason...

Having no alternative, we ourselves watched over the property of the Jewish Agency until daybreak, when we discovered Noga, actually under our noses!

The village of Noga, where we made our home, could be called the village of "old settlers". As opposed to the other settlers of the Lachish region, who had come "from ship to settlement", the settlers of Noga were drawn from the various *ma'abarot*. The first settlers were eleven families from Iran, who had come from the Agrobank *ma'abara*, and ourselves, a single family from Kfar Warburg. The families who had come from the *ma'abarot* already knew Hebrew, and knew how to complain fluently. Their constant complaints were the distinguishing mark of those who had come from the *ma'abarot*. For longer than half a year the village, with its dozen families, existed under very bad security conditions, due solely to the fact that the Agency workers could not convince the many inhabitants of the *ma'abarot* to leave their 'paradise' of crowded tin huts. However, it must be admitted that the vast area without the semblance of a building, and the tiny huts erected at some distance from one other, had nothing in them to encourage the people to leave the well-populated *ma'abara* and the busy highway and move to the Lachish region.

The first night in Noga was a dark night, at the end of the month of Tammuz. The Government Information Bureau was concerned about the morale of the new settlers, and made an attempt to cheer them up. They sent us a singer and an accordion-player to "raise our spirits". One of the young men of Noga later told me humorously of the impression the performance that evening made on him:

"... Outside, it was black as Egypt, and the glass chimney of the kerosene lamp broke. All right, so we have to get used to sleeping in the dark! All of a sudden a horn honks, and the instructor calls out: 'Everybody bring benches!' The people are tired, they want to go to sleep, and for that matter, how many were we, anyhow? But we all came out, and we brought a *lux,* a gasoline lantern. The singer came out and began to warble in a thin voice. What's she doing here? Honestly, I felt sorry for her: a lady who'd come down from her third-floor flat in Tel Aviv, and for what?..."

Today the settlers of Noga, Shakhar, and the other villages of the area come to their common Recreation Centre — a magnificent building, filled with light — to film showings and performances of the local dramatic group, or other entertainments. Today the story I was told sounds like a fairy tale, but all this actually happened five years ago...

X

SERVANTS OF THE PEOPLE

IN THE CENTER of the new Ashkelon two long rows of Swedish pre-fabs were erected, where all the people working on the settlement project of the new region were concentrated: architects, draughtsmen, surveyors, and other technicians. In addition to these, there were also the coordinators of instruction for the villages, and their advisory staff — experienced anthropologists and sociologists. This was the first time that people in the various branches of absorption, immigration, planning, and construction were working together as a closely coordinated team.

The work was carried out very rapidly. There were periods when the planning authorities determined the rate as one settlement per week. The Yarkon River pipeline, laying of the railroad track which cuts across the Lachish region on the way to Beer Sheva, the construction of large factories, the excavation of Lake Zohar, the paving of a network of highways where there had never even been a trace of a road. Visitors today find it hard to believe that the development of the region was begun only in 1955.

During one year alone (December 1954 — December 1955) these settlements were planned and founded: the new immigrant city, Kiryat-Gat, and twenty agricultural settlements of new immigrants from Eastern countries, three settlements of Nakhal near the Hebron border, two settlements of Israeli youth, two agricultural training farms and two village centres. During the same year, the cotton gin was also built in Kiryat-gat, and the foundation laid for a modern spinning factory.

The planning and settlement authorities tried to apply the lessons of their previous experience, and the settlement project of the Lachish region was given unprecedented attention by the various government departments and public authorities. They strove to prevent any unnecessary discomfort being suffered by the settlers, and to correct or reduce the errors made in all the previous settlement projects. Everything to which the new settler was entitled was given to him immediately, or at the soonest possible opportunity.

There was 20 workers in "headquarters", most of them young people. The few older people took their places among them and did their work modestly. The difficult task of directing all the work was done by a very young man, who was slight and fair-haired, quiet and polite. There was something ascetic in his character — "like fire in the bones". His name was Aryeh Eliav, but he was always addressed by his nickname, 'Lyova'. Lyova had formerly been the secretary of Levi Eshkol, who described him in one of his pungent remarks: "I need a secretary who is both an orphan and a widower, and that's what Lyova is, even though he has a mother, a wife, and children."

It should be added that Lyova is a good son, a faithful husband, and a devoted father; but for him, everything is woven into the fabric of his work. It is difficult to compress his rich biography into the number of years of his life. Born in Russia, he attended the 'Herzlia' high school, was an officer in the British army, an organizer of the illegal immigration bringing shiploads of illegal immigrants, a lieutenant-colonel in the Israeli army, and assistant to the Head of the Jewish Agency's Agricultural Department. He studied farm management in England, and from the beginning of the settlement project in the Lachish region, he was its first director. Afterwards, he completed Hebrew University and became the First Secretary of the Embassy of Israel in Moscow. Today Aryeh Eliav is the director of the settlement project in the Arad region.

His office was unique — its doors were always wide open. Tea drinking by the clerks during working hours was forbidden, and when necessary there was a night shift. Most of the clerks wore khaki to work. When furniture was ordered for the offices of the region headquarters, Lyova announced that he preferred desks without drawers: "When you have drawers," he would explain, "you put papers into them, and as a result, lots of the papers simply get overlooked."

Lyova had time for everything, and especially for visits to the villages, talks and personal ties with the settlers. And another fact should be mentioned: since Lyova liked to learn everything from his own experience, he had gone to be an instructor in Nevatim, a village of new immigrants from Cochin near Beer Sheva, before his appointment as regional head. He stayed there over a year, and even transferred a few families from Nevatim to Shakhar, one of the villages of Lachish. To this day, if you want to dispel a cloud from the face of one of the immigrants from Cochin, it is enough to mention the name "Lyova".

During the trying times experienced by the Lachish region before the Sinai Campaign, when there was a great increase in border incidents and every road might have an ambush set up by infiltrators, Lyova would reach the Lachish settlements in the middle of the night, travelling with an army patrol on top of a half-track. On the bulletin board, together with announcements and news bulletins, there was a notice bearing these words :

> "Let us all remember that when we come into contact with the village instructors, the farm managers and their secretaries and with the settlers themselves, we must behave politely, patiently, and with as quick a response as possible. We will do well to understand that the work of those on the front line, inside the villages, is hard, monotonous, and filled with complications, and that our function is to *serve them,* to make things easier for them, and to help them in carrying out their duties."
>
> Signed: A. Eliav

The first people we met when we arrived in Noga were the two instructors, a young man and a woman. These instructors arrived in every village together with the modest equipment sent for the houses of the settlers by the Jewish Agency: beds, a table, a kerosene camp stove, and a small supply of food. The instructor was always the first to greet the new settler, and more than once the impression made by the instructor has determined, to a considerable degree, the new immigrant's attitude to his new home.

The Hebrew word for 'instructor' also means 'guide', and it became a common term in Israel when the settlement of the new immigrant villages began.

First to volunteer to serve as instructors for the new immigrant villages, were the older settlers from agricultural settlements. In 1954, they were replaced by the younger generation from the *moshavim* (smallholders' cooperative villages like Kfar Warburg and Beer Tuvia) who responded to Ben Gurion's appeal for volunteers. However, the young people were unable to serve for longer than two years, as their own farms could not continue to operate for an extended period of time in their absence. Experience showed that the success of the guidance depended to a great extent on the continual presence of the instructors in their respective villages for as prolonged a period as possible; but the settlement administration was unable to achieve this goal. Only very few of the instructors, men or women, stayed in one village longer than two years. As a result of this lack of constant and regular guidance, relations between the settlement administration and the settlers suffered from misunderstandings on both sides.

Despite this routine problem, it must be pointed out that the success of the settlement project in Lachish was due primarily to three factors: strict adherence to the predetermined time schedule; expert planning and coordination between the planning bodies and the operating headquarters at a local level; and most important — provision of regular work for the settlers during the period before their land began to produce.

The implementation of these principles was the job of the

instructors. In the settlement of Lachish, emphasis was put on guidance, and especially on agricultural instruction. The Agency spared no expense when it seemed advisable to assign to a new village two, or even three, agricultural instructors. Funds were not wasted on items of lesser importance, such as permanent farm buildings and the like; they were used, rather, to prepare large areas of irrigated land for every settler, in order to create a source of income for him. The land was not immediately turned over to its owners; the individual owner first learned how to work land by working on it as a hired labourer. This arrangement had many advantages, among them: The settler's full employment in productive work and not 'relief works', and his learning how to farm with no financial risk. The instructors employed the farm owner until he adapted himself to agricultural work and himself requested to undertake the responsibility of running his own farm.

To the agricultural instructors in every village were added other professional workers: a teacher, a kindergarten teacher, a practical nurse, managers and supervisors in various fields. Together these formed a "team", on whose organization and coordination depended, to a great extent, the success of the entire project. The goal of the team was to help the man torn out of his native surroundings root himself in the country and in the life of the nation.

However, as yet no one knew exactly how to attain this goal. In order to be a shoemaker, one must first be a shoemaker's apprentice. But there was no institution to train instructors. The government did not have enough time to set up training schools for instructors, and more than once vital responsibilities were placed on the shoulders of people chosen at random, in hopes that they would learn how to swim when they were tossed into the sea...

Ways and means regarded as suitable in the past were discovered to be unsuitable under the new conditions. The urgency of the task at hand did not permit debate and lengthy consideration. Members of the team of village workers learned as they worked, often through their own errors.

The instructor was always the first target for the arrows of resentment and criticism. If wages were late in being paid — hadn't the instructor stolen the money? And if the distribution of work seemed unfair to someone — wasn't it obvious that the instructor was giving *'proteksia'* (playing favourites)? Thus the background was prepared for accusations and recriminations.

The constant turnover of instructors made their work even harder: a young man would show up full of energy, ready to remake the world, — while he himself was of completely unstable character. And before an opportunity arose for him to demonstrate his powers, he was already gone with the wind. The instructor who would take his place might be in total disagreement with his predecessor's methods, and introduce conflicting methods of his own; and the perplexed settler would cease to place faith in *any* instructor.

Even more difficult was the work of the woman instructor, whose main goal was to overcome the isolation of the new woman settler and help her adapt to the conditions of her new life. More than once a young girl, who had herself never either managed a household or cared for children, would — while trying to carry out her responsibilities as an instructor — give ridiculously self-confident advice to some woman who had raised a dozen well-behaved children and who had enough experience in managing her household to be capable of keeping a supply of food for an almost unlimited time with no refrigeration facilities. Moreover, the children of the new immigrant had been brought up to be polite and to show respect to their parents and other older people, which was not always the case with the Israeli-bred young woman instructor...

Friction with the instructors — apparently for no justifiable reason — was a frequent occurrence in the history of the new settlements in the country. Nor did the settlers always content themselves with purely verbal disagreement. The second year we were in Lachish, the agricultural instructor of one of the villages was brought to us unconscious and suffering from a severe beating. Four of the settlers had attacked him while he was alone in the fields and had beaten him unmercifully. The young man understood their grievances and made no charges, for against whom should he bring suit? ...

In 1954 an incident occurred which opened the country's eyes to the value and meaning of the instructors' work. The death of Varda Friedman, a daughter of Kfar Vitkin who was murdered by infiltrators during an attack on a wedding celebration in Kfar Patish, shocked the public and drew attention to the devoted work of the instructors, men and women.

I was well-acquainted with Patish, I had visited there several times before the tragedy. The settlers of the village were immigrants from Kurdistan who had frequently been described as quarrelsome and violent. After Varda's death, however, there was a change in these people. They all showed a deep concern for the safety of the women instructors and teachers, and would not permit them to leave their houses in the evenings.

One of the settlers said to the woman instructor: "You don't have to come visit us in the evening. You be careful about yourself, that's more important."

One day when I was visiting in Patish, one of the Agency officials came to the village. He shook my hand, and with great respect kissed the hand of the young woman instructor. "We must show our respect for the daughters of the *moshavim!*" he remarked to the embarrassed young woman.

Among the things that increased the settlers' respect for the young people from the *moshavim,* and also set an example for them, was the courage of the young instructors from the *moshavim.* In Patish I once found the village instructor, a boy from Kfar Vitkin, tossing in his bed, both his feet wrapped in bandages. When I asked him how he had been injured, he told me that one night infiltrators came and stole the pipes. This was nothing new in that area: ever since the Agency had begun distributing irrigation pipes made of aluminum to the villages, the operations of the thieves who crossed the border every night had become far easier. The watchmen would fire a few shots at the infiltrators and leave it at that. After all, the pipes belonged to the Agency: if they were stolen — others would be given out. And was it worth risking your life for them? ...

But the pride of the young man from Kfar Vitkin rebelled against this slavish attitude towards the insolent robbers from across the border, and he decided to end the "sport" of stealing irrigation pipes. When he heard the watchman's shots that night, he jumped from his bed and chased the infiltrators several kilometres, until they dropped the pipes and left the way they had come.

In his haste, the young instructor had pulled sandals onto his bare feet.

"It's a pity!" he said sadly. "They wouldn't have gotten away from me if I'd been wearing shoes. It's fall now, and all the fields are ploughed, and the hard clods really 'killed' my feet..."

Everyone was filled with admiration for the work of an older couple from the *kvutza* of Ginegar, who were later joined by an experienced nurse from Yarkona. The three of them worked with the settlers of Kfar Otsem for two years, from the day the group arrived in the country. The influence of their work can be seen to this day, in the high standards of hygiene among the women of Otsem, and in the settlers' attitude of respect for the instructors and other members of the village team.

The outstanding quality in the work of these elderly instructors was the degree of tact and tolerance they showed in presenting their ideas, and their sincere respect for the ideas and beliefs of the immigrants themselves. In their small hut the village workers became a united team, and thence flowed the spirit of devotion and willingness to do hard work — an honourable tradition indeed!

I was filled with admiration for the liberal attitude of the woman instructor in Kfar Otsem when she was confronted with sights that are generally intolerable to the European eye. Both she and her house shone with cleanliness, yet in winter she would allow the small children in the village to go around in their long dresses, barefoot, and without underpants.

"Their mothers," she explained to me, "have had experience themselves. My grandson has two dozen pairs of long pants, and he can be changed whenever necessary, but here a child would walk around in wet pants all day, until he caught cold or got a rash..."

I wanted to include her in the project to provide rubber boots to the children in kindergarten, but she refused, and contended:

"Other things are more important. The children from Morocco have never worn rubber boots in their lives. They don't feel the necessity for it, because they're used to going barefoot. The mud doesn't stick to a bare foot the way it does to a rubber boot. We have to be patient and wait till they learn to wear them."

How right she was I discovered when I distributed shiny new rubber boots to the kindergarten children in Noga. The children plodded through the mud with the greatest difficulty until they got tired of it, and in the end they would leave the rubber boots wherever they happened to be and draw a breath of relief at ridding themselves of the uncomfortable encumbrance.

The first words in Hebrew the women of Otsem learned from their instructor were: "soap and water." In the beginning, some of them were innocently convinced that this was the name of the instructor.

In the nurse's hut, the two women of the team kept and raised a poor girl baby. The baby was two weeks old when her mother fell ill and was taken to the hospital. The family "gave up" the infant, for what value has a girl child in the eyes of the East, and who would take care of it while its mother was in the hospital? But how great was the family rejoicing when the mother came home and her little girl was returned to her safe and sound!

The general instructor, from Ginegar, could "do anything", as far as the villagers were concerned.

— "Ask the instructor, he knows!..."

One of the reasons for the faith and trust placed in this elderly couple from Ginegar was, perhaps, the fact that they themselves were religious, and observers of traditional customs, as were the new settlers.

In the house of the couple from Ginegar is a sheet of parchment, with the following inscription in Rashi script, written by the aged rabbi of the village of Otsem on the day they left:

> Through the divine attributes of wisdom and grace:
> He who blessed our forefathers twice,
> Because of Adam and his two sons,
> Because of Abraham of Aram-Naharaim,
> Because of Isaac between the altar's horns,

Because of Jacob who conquered Machanaim,
Because of Joseph who went down to Mezraim,
Because of Moses who brought the Torah down from heaven,
Because of Aaron who sacrificed at even,
Because of Rabbi Shimeon who composed the Book of Zohar,
Because of David who made psalms with song and cymbal,
Because of Israel who went forth six hundred thousand —

May God above bless and watch over and aid and enlarge and raise up the great and lofty and honourable Bezalel Nehorai, may his candle burn high. May the Lord shield him from every sorrow and distress, amen, may this be the Lord's will, he and his honourable wife the lady Ahuva, may the Lord protect her and support her, they and their sons and all their seed. Amen, may this be the Lord's will.

The composer of this ancient traditional prayer from the Atlas mountains certainly never imagined in what fashion and by what paths his prayer would reach Ginegar.

XI

OUR FIRST DAYS IN NOGA

WE MADE OUR home in Noga. This village had its own specific problems, and the most difficult was the re-education of the people themselves. The years they had spent in various *ma'abarot* were not the most suitable training for life in an agricultural settlement.

Several days before we moved our belongings to Noga, I went there with my two daughters to see the tiny house where we would live. The houses were temporary wooden huts, and several young men were engaged in painting them.

"Where are you from?" I asked.

"From the Agrobank *ma'abara*. We're going to live here."

"We'll be neighbours, then. We're going to live here, too."

"And what about the girls?"

"They'll live with us, too."

"Oh. And you'll go home on the Sabbath?"

"We won't go anywhere. This is going to be our home."

One of the young men made a face and whistled impudently. I thought to myself at the time that I wouldn't care to meet him alone at night on the road. This same young man has served through the years as the driver for the Area Council, and has become a faithful friend of the family.

We could not move our belongings to Lachish all at once, although even in Kfar Warburg we did not possess a large amount of furniture. Taking into consideration the measurements of the small hut, we took with us only the most necessary furnishings.

The one piece of furniture I simply could not give up was our large table, which took up almost half the area of the house. However, it served as a most useful piece of furniture: around this table were held almost all the meetings, debates, quarrels and reconciliations during the first months of the settlement of Lachish. This table also made it possible for us to turn the house into a dining hall for a good number of people, and perhaps this was its most important function in those days.

Baruch, our neighbour from Kfar Warburg, came with us and helped us get settled on our first day in our new home. When we arrived in the truck loaded with our belongings, the village team of workers — the general instructor, a young woman instructor, and a practical nurse — came over to introduce themselves. Looking at them, it seemed to me that my own age was greater than the combined ages of all three.

I asked them where they lived and how they had gotten settled. The three exchanged significant glances. It turned out that the team had been sent to the village two days before the arrival of the settlers. The small tin hut, which was supposed to serve as a cooperative kitchen, still lacked all the basic equipment. The Yarkon pipeline had not yet been connected to the "Lachishes" and drinking water was piped through a very small pipeline from one of the kibbutzim in the south. Faucets had not yet been installed in the huts, and water had to be carried in buckets from the center of the village. The village store had not yet been opened. Generally speaking, the team was living a 'pioneering' life.

Baruch helped us unload the table — the first piece of furniture placed in the house. We ate our first meal in Noga with a *'minyan'* of guests, and this seemed to us a good omen for the future.

The first young woman instructor vanished after a few days, and the general instructor brought another young woman to our house, whom I shall call Rina, though that is not her name. He remarked that she was a university student who had volunteered to instruct new immigrants during her month's vacation.

This young woman made an unforgettable impression with her education and her intelligence. She did not tell us her family name or where she worked, or anything at all about herself. I suggested that she take her midday meal with us, so she would be able to utilize fully the little time she had. She accepted my proposal willingly. I saw her, therefore, every day of that month, and I learned that she was the daughter of a family from Salonika, a chemist with university education, who had attained her position through her own efforts. Rina devoted most of her attention to the care of one family with many children, immigrants from Iran. The elderly father was unable to support the family. The mother was weak and overburdened with work. The children went around half naked and looked as though they had never in their lives had enough to eat.

Rina visited the family every day, and took part in its daily life: she helped the mother cook, launder, and care for the children. Once she came to me with the proposal that I too take part in her project: she had succeeded in gaining the favour of the father of the family and he had given her twenty pounds in cash for clothing for the half-dozen small children who went around barefoot and almost naked. As this sum was not enough to buy ready-made clothes, Rina approached me with the request that I help her sew clothes for them.

I was filled with respect for this capable young woman. The children's father had told me that they had been better off in the *ma'abara*, and claimed that the Jewish Agency was supposed to provide clothing for the children of new immigrants. He also claimed that he had spoken personally to Golda about this question of "policy", and she had confirmed that he was not responsible for clothing the children.

Rina travelled to nearby Migdal and bought khaki cloth with the entire sum. She asked me to cut the cloth as sparingly as possible, so that every child should receive at least one shirt and one pair of pants that fitted him.

I was glad I had one useful talent. During all my years in the country, I have sewn myself all the clothing required by my family. I asked Rina to bring me the battalion of urchins so that I could measure them. Together with the "battalion" came the "commander", the father of the family, who was already filled with remorse that in a moment of weakness he had allowed a scheming woman to beguile him and get twenty pounds in hard cash out of him. He measured the material over and over, arguing with Rina about the quantity and the price, in order to demonstrate that he too knew quite a bit about matters like these.

He supervised every move I made as I marked and cut the material, giving me the benefit of his advice the entire time. Finally he counted the cut-out garments again, collected the leftover scraps of cloth, and left angrily.

At night I worked by the light of the kerosene lamp. The air was stifling; the windows were blacked out, for our house stood on the edge of the wadi, and the wadi was a natural place of concealment for infiltrators. Rina came every day and praised my ability and my quickness as a seamstress. She promised to sew the buttons and buttonholes herself. When they were finished, I gave her the bundle of clothes; but that was not the end of the affair.

For some reason or other, Rina was delayed in making the buttonholes; but the angry father continued to pursue me. He would come to me every day to demand that I give him either the clothes or the money. To his way of thinking, he should have been given both...

Meanwhile the days of Rina's vacation drew to a close, and her work as an instructor in the village came to an end. She left Lachish enveloped in the gratitude and admiration of both the settlers and the team of village workers. The instructor collected money from everyone, and we gave Rina a present to remember us by.

And again the bundle of clothes came back to me. I made the buttonholes as well, and brought the clothes to their owners, to cover their nakedness. The father measured and inspected every detail with his own hands, and began to criticise and censure my professional ability:

"— No good! This is too small, and this is too short... there was plenty of material, and what did you do with it? We're "blacks" and you don't care how well you do anything for us!..."

I gave him a bundle of whatever I could lay my hands on, and that was my undoing — for over a year, the man gave me no rest: he continually demanded his "change" from me, and each time he got another present out of me.

The man's neighbours scolded me. In the course of time, I learned that they were right. They told me that they knew the man before he had come to the country, from the city where he originated. He was known to be rich and miserly. Without a doubt — said the neighbours — he had a hoard of riches with him, but he also had "lots of sense" and he always tried to cheat anyone who wasn't as smart as he was...

Long afterwards I read the story of Ida Priver, a village instructor. Among other things, she described an incident deserving the attention of anyone who sets out to bridge the gap between two different cultures. At the beginning of the mass immigration, Ida Priver worked in a village of Yemenites. In the beginning, the Yemenite women refused to give birth in hospitals. When the woman instructor went to visit one of them the morning after she had given birth, she found the new mother doing laundry. Here is Ida Priver's description of the incident:

"... I ordered Shoshanna to get into bed. I immediately called her neighbours and asked them to help her with the housework until she was well. I explained to them the meaning of mutual aid, and how useful it could be to any one of them if, God forbid, she should fall ill. The women stared at me with a total lack of understanding. Why should they help? Every one of them did her own housework, whatever the state of her health, with no help at all. They stood there without saying a word, and not one of them moved from her place.

"Beside the tub was a heap of dirty clothes. I sat down on the stool and started to work. I knew that I had to prove myself, to set an example...

"... The next day I went to Shoshanna's house again. I found her busy in the kitchen. She was expecting me: "Here, instructor," she said, pointing at a pile of dirty clothes in the corner. "The soap and the tubs are outside. You can do the laundry, everything's all ready for you..."

We arrived in Lachish-3 (today Noga) at the beginning of the summer vacation, before the huts which were to serve as a school were furnished. But the young people's clubhouse was already furnished with tables and benches, and various youth instructors appeared — most of them university students who came to work during the summer.

Full employment was available for all the settlers of the Lachish region, and not "relief work." This was one of the greatest achievements of the planning of Lachish. Every man who was able to work was employed in the construction of the houses, paving of the roads, ditch-digging, putting up fences, and planting trees. For this reason, programs for the youth took place only in the evenings; the clubhouse was empty during the day. There, together with my daughter, I collected the few children of the village, all of whom were wandering about in rags and tatters and were utterly filthy, and we kept them as busy as we could.

This village, which drew its population from the already existing *ma'abarot,* was filled only with difficulty: a *ma'abara* is not like a ship-ful of immigrants. It was impossible to remove people from a *ma'abara* by order and arbitrarily send them to a new settlement.

We settled Noga with eleven families, and this was our total population for three months, until unexpected "reinforcements" arrived from Tiberias. They arrived as the result of a fearful riot among the occupants of the Tiberias *ma'abara,* which broke out on a holiday when "their hearts were merry with wine." Approximately a thousand people took part in the riot, which continued for two days without stopping. Only with great difficulty did the police get the situation under control and isolate the firebrands, who were subsequently resettled in widely separated places.

In this way the first families of Iraqi immigrants arrived in Noga, creating a background for friction with the original settlers, immigrants from Iran. The families from Tiberias had a multitude of children, whose neglect was quite apparent. However, they brought with them a definite way of life, and they were learned in Torah and tradition. One of their elders was a man respected by all, the moral guide and leader of his community. With the arrival of the Iraqis, a competition began between the two communities in Noga, and each group tried to attract to Noga their relations, who were in various *ma'abarot* throughout the country.

Mordecai was swamped with work. There was an urgent need for organizing the educational and health services, and for regularizing municipal affairs. The village centre, which was to serve all the villages of Lachish and provide all the necessary services, existed meanwhile only on the map; it indeed required careful and farsighted planning, for it was to be the prototype, the first village centre in the country. The large table in our house served as an office for the Lachish Area Council for some time before the Minister of the Interior officially recognized the Council's existence.

After Rina left the village, T'nuat Hamoshavim sent a permanent woman instructor, who was also very young. I personally saw no opportunity at all of being employed as a public servant in any capacity. My one comfort was the two dozen children who had grown attached to me and came to me for lessons day after day. Then Aryeh Simon arrived in Noga. Aryeh Simon was the supervisor of schools in the south and the Negev, whom I had previously met many times during the period when I was working with the libraries in the Negev.

When he asked me how I was and what I was doing, I was completely frank. I told him that meanwhile I had had no success in finding occupation for myself.

"You haven't got a job?" he exclaimed, as though it were a pleasant surprise. "Come to the school! I've been tearing my hair out trying to figure out how to get enough young women soldiers to volunteer for teaching in the new Lachish Settlements. The villages here are sprouting up like mushrooms."

In my heart, I had been hoping for this offer. No other job, no matter how important or respected, attracted me as much Simon's offer at the time.

I shall always recall with nostalgia the first year we spent in Noga. Living side by side with the settlers of the village, the close contact with them, the affectionate relations with my pupils which sprang up despite the problems of working under bad housing conditions and with mixed grades in the classroom — all these forged the bonds of an unalterable attachment to the village.

Just before Rosh Hashana, Noga had two distinguished visitors — President Ben-Zvi and his wife, who are known for having a 'weak spot' for huts and their occupants.

The heads of the eleven familes of Noga assembled at our house. The President had to bend his head a little in order to go through the doorway of the hut, but it seemed to me at the time that the ceiling raised itself when he entered. The settlers greeted him, according to their custom, with the prayer 'He Who has Blessed' and answered his questions respectfully.

This is the story that the President of the State of Israel told in the old hut that had been moved to Noga from one of the *ma'abarot* and served as our house:

"... On my trip to Iran, I reached the city of Demavind, in the valley of Gilerad. I discovered that the valley was once settled by the men of Gilead, after their exile from Eretz-Israel, and the valley was named after them. In the days of Ezra, the valley was populated by a large and flourishing Jewish community. Ezra suggested to them that they return to Israel, but they refused, claiming that it was unsafe in Eretz-Israel and they would be better off to remain in the Persian exile. Ezra said to them: "You are many now, but the day will come when you are few. Today your fate is in your own hands. Tomorrow, perhaps, things may be otherwise..."

"The Jews of the valley of Gilerad did not heed his call. And indeed, in the course of time, they became very few, until only a handful were left and around them a huge graveyard. The remnants of these few families have only now returned to the country — and God grant that the entire nation learn the historic lesson..."

In token of his visit, the President gave the first Persian community in Lachish the Torah scroll of a Jewish community in Iran which once numbered 14,000 souls. The same city had now been emptied of its Jews. The last to leave took with them the Torah scrolls and presented them to the President of the State of Israel, and he took care that these Torah scrolls return to the hands of Jews who came from Iran.

The Torah follows its followers...

That historic day for the Lachish region ended with a festive luncheon. The President and his wife took Mordecai and myself to this luncheon, which was served in Metsudat Yoav — the police station of Iraq-Suidan, near Negba, where Nasser was once entrenched, and which was nicknamed during the War of Independence "The Monster on the Hill".

Fate willed that I be faced with this police station every day for these five years, when I open the door of my house in the morning. I have not yet grown accustomed to the idea that this "Monster" is a building exactly like all the other police stations in the country, and that it is ours. Whenever I go near it, to the deserted, shadeless yard, the shell-riddled walls with peeling plaster, I am overcome by a feeling of 'Put off thy shoe...'

The luncheon was held in honour of the hero of the conquest of Nitsana, Aluf Maier Amit. Only fourteen people were present, most of them army men, famed for their exploits. The modest table was set up in a small room. The meal was served by one soldier in uniform. When the guests were called to the table, the food was already waiting, and the glasses already filled with wine. Suddenly Rachel Ben Zvi rose and said, with deep feeling:

"How can we eat here, in this place, without first saying a prayer and recalling that everything — the bread, the oil and the wine — all this is *theirs*..."

We stood around the table in silent prayer.

I wrote down another prayer for myself on the work schedule at the beginning of the new year — the first year of our life in the Lachish region. It was the prayer of a farmer:

'Lord, when I build my home, make my nights shorter and my days longer.'

XII

A CHANGE OF CLIMATE

The people of Israel have known how to create an educational climate in all the countries of their exile. I once heard Dr. Yom-Tov Levinsky tell how a small child would be taken for the first time to the house of his rabbi in a village in Galicia fifty years ago. The date was set for Shavuot, on the holiday of the Presentation of the Torah. The age of the beginners was between three and four years, "when the child knows how to speak". The pupil would bathe and be purified in a *mikveh* after a night of vigil. His mother would dress the child in new clothes, and his father would wrap him completely in a *talith* — a prayer shawl — (that he might not see on the way a pig, a drunkard, or any other impure sight), and would carry him to the synagogue on his shoulder. There they would seat the new pupils in a row, and the rabbi would repeat the verse: "*Moses commanded us a law, an inheritance of the congregation of Jacob*", until they knew it by heart. He would then show them a tablet on which the letters of the alphabet were written. The tablet was spread with honey. The rabbi read out the letters and would let the children touch them and lick their fingers, as if to say: *the Torah is sweeter than honey*. At the same time, an 'angel' would shower sweets on them from above.

In the late afternoon the children would be brought to the Rabbi again, this time to his house, where they would begin their regular studies. The *melamed* would take them for a walk, usually on the banks of a river. The children would crumble bread and throw crumbs into the water to feed the fish. In this way, the rabbi would give his pupils their first moral instruction: "*One must not beat a dog, or chase a cat — be kind to dumb animals!*"...

People from Yemen and Morocco tell similar stories. The difference is that in their countries, this tradition has been carried on to this day. There is great perturbation among the Eastern immigrants at present. They are fearful of the results of modern education, and they ask in concern: "What kind of education is this that forbids one to chastise a child who has done wrong? And how is it that a woman is permitted to do the teaching?"

The campaign for education has been no easier for the State of Israel than the military campaigns in which we gained victory. People say that the officers of the Israeli army are in the habit of commanding their troops with the words: "After me!", instead of "Forward!" — and that this is the secret of their success. But the state of affairs in the field of education bears no resemblance to the traditional behaviour of the army. In this field, it is mainly the beginners and teachers with no experience at all who are sent to the "firing lines," while most of the experienced and well-trained teachers entrench themselves in well-protected flanking positions.

When the settlement of Lachish began, public education had already gone a long way since its inception. The standard of studies has risen in all the training institutions, and today qualified teachers are sent to almost every isolated spot. This was not the case ten years ago. As an example, here is an advertisement in a daily newspaper of February, 1953. The advertisers did not seek or demand, but pleaded and begged for mercy:

> "What teacher, male or female, is prepared to volunteer for at least this school year to teach in the Eilat public school, and by doing so, to enable the local school to exist"...

The "righteous man" is assured of his wage in this world as well as the next, but he is in no hurry to present himself... At that time, the supervisor of schools in the Negev returned from Eilat. He told me about the paralysis of the school, and concluded with a dramatic appeal:

"Would you like your name to be inscribed on the gates of Eilat as one of its founders and builders? If you would, get us some kind of teacher — any kind, as long as he's honest and a Jew. In all, there are 16 children in Eilat. Let him keep them busy in any way he wants! Otherwise, all the decent people will leave Eilat. Who'll agree to live in a city that can't provide a teacher for its children?..."

In my travels to the villages of the Negev, I once spent the night in the home of a Yemenite. I wanted to test the reading knowledge of the nine-year-old son, and I corrected his errors as he read. Suddenly his father interfered determinedly:

"Why are you teaching the boy everything wrong? You say 'chashuv' instead of 'khashuv', 'biglal' instead of 'bichlal'. You turn everything upside down! It is forbidden to pronounce the letters however you choose. We must pronounce them exactly as Moshe gave them to us on Mount Sinai!..."

As a member of a community that tended the faint ember with such devotion, a community dedicated in its study of the Torah, this traditional Yemenite could not bear the "falsifying" of the sacred tongue on the lips of a woman from the Ashkenazi community who mispronounced the original accent. I was embarrassed and ashamed.

I left his house with his two sons. The eldest, who was about thirteen, took me in the wagon to the neighbouring village, while the younger son, with whom I had been talking in the house, sat beside me. In the course of our conversation during the trip, I learned that the elder brother had already quit school.

"The teachers are no good," he claimed. "They're lazy... it's a waste of time... I'm better off helping out on the farm..."

"Do you still remember the way you studied in Yemen?"

"Of course! We sat on the floor around the book, and we all read."

I asked him several questions about the Bible, and found that he did, indeed, recall even the precise wording. Then I turned to his nine-year-old brother.

"And what part of the Bible are you studying in school?"
"Genesis."
"And do you remember what you studied this year?"
"Certainly!"
"How many patriarchs were there?"
(An embarrassed silence).
"You just didn't understand my question," I said. "I mean Abraham, Isaac, and Jacob. Have you heard of them?"
"Of course!"
"And was Abraham Isaac's father, or was Isaac Abraham's father?"
"Isaac was Abraham's father."
"Are you certain of that?"
"Of course!"

I tried to persuade him of his error, but he remained unconvinced. He had only a vague concept of Biblical genealogy. He did not know the difference between Esau and Ishmael, or between Noah and Lot. He seemed to be hearing most of the Biblical names I mentioned for the first time. I was astonished by this, for the boy's father was a scholar. However, the elder brother explained the riddle:

"It's shameful to learn Torah from a woman! Torah that you learn like that doesn't get into your head..."

Every year the days of school registration are days of torment in the so-called "development areas". The atmosphere of "proselytizing" that sweeps the country during general elections to the Knesset can be encountered every year in the homes of new immigrants whose children have just reached school age. The children, too, learn to exploit this situation...

During the first two years of Kiryat-Gat's existence, two schools, the religious school and the public school, were crowded into huts that shared the same lot. The two schools had a common dining-hall. One of the school principals told me of cases where a pupil wanted to "punish " his teacher. All he had to do to accomplish this was to go out into the hall, hang up his tiny skullcap on a hook and start attending the public school; or the opposite — to take the skullcap from its hook and put it on...

Five years ago I chanced to walk through the forest of huts in the *ma'abara* of Migdal. I had already lost hope of finding the address I sought, but a ten-year-old little girl volunteered to guide me.

While we were walking, I asked her, "What grade are you in?"

"Fourth grade."

"And what is your class studying?"

"We study everything: Hebrew, science, math — I've got twelve notebooks!" She smiled and added: "I used to be in sixth grade, but I didn't like it, so I left."

"How is it that you were in sixth grade?" I asked in surprise. "You don't look as though you're old enough."

"That's the way things are. In the "Aguda", they put me into sixth grade, and I've only got two pair of pants — a summer pair, and a winter pair. The teacher told me 'Aren't you ashamed of yourself?', so I left and went to "public"..."

Thus lightly do the children decide to attend one school or the other. This is not true of the parents: many of them feel themselves completely lost with the collapse of religious and traditional values. The lack of courtesy which has become usual among children of Eastern immigrants since they have been in the country shocks their elders, and is an evil portent to them. Nor do they find comfort in the fact that the children learn far more.

"What has he learned," they ask, "if he does not know how to honour his father and mother? He will not even know how to say '*kaddish*' for us..."

I once spoke tactlessly and remarked to one of the elders

of Noga, a man of tradition and a figure of influence in his community, that the little children of the village were neglected and turned out into the street. This was after an incident in which his small grandson had been almost miraculously saved from death.

The old man replied, "And you neglect your old parents and turn them out, is that good? The child doesn't know that he is neglected, but the old man — he knows, he knows..."

"In Proverbs," he added, "it is written: *Honor thy Lord with thy substance*, which is to say: you must give the gleanings, the corners and the tenth part of your substance; but if you have none, there is no obligation. But you are commanded to support your father, even if you must go begging from door to door..."

Thus was the old man from Kurdistan trained, and he brought a complete set of moral values with him from that undeveloped country. It is not his fault that he has been unable to inculcate this mode of conduct in his son.

Pioneers of education in the Lachish region were the graduates of the seminars — privates in the army and beginners in the field of teaching. On their young shoulders rested the heavy responsibility of educating the younger generation that would be rooted in the soil of Lachish.

One of the parents said pessimistically: "They've come here to practise giving a haircut on the head of an orphan..."

Nevertheless, there is no question but that without them, the situation would have been far worse. The very fact of the teachers' living in the villages of Lachish during the first year was a brave act, and is to their credit.

At that time the entire population of Lachish was living in temporary huts, and the Torah was also housed in a hut. According to the plan, a regional school for seven villages was going to be built in Nehora. During this first year two teachers were sent to every village, to teach the children in all grades together. In none of the villages of Lachish, with the exception of Noga, did the children know a word of Hebrew, and the teachers were forced to learn several dialects of French and Arabic in order to create some kind of channel of communication between themselves and their pupils.

As for me, there was a special kind of magic in the poor hut of the first school in Noga, a magic I did not succeed in transplanting to the orderly, well-equipped school in the village centre, with its spacious, well-decorated classrooms. Perhaps it was the missing smiles of the Persian and Kurdish mothers in Noga that kept me company every morning on my way to work. As a rule, the smile we exchanged was the sole expression of mutual understanding, for we had no common language at all.

The school in Noga occupied two huts which stood next to one another. The children were divided, according to age, between myself and a girl soldier-teacher. Once, during recess, I was standing near the hut where the young teacher taught. Her lesson was still in progress, and she was repeating in a chorus with her pupils the multiplication tables. The children read rhythmically:

"Two times four are eight! Two times five are ten! Two times six are twelve!"

An old woman passed by; she was wrapped in layers of rags, with her hair dressed in braids and curls, after the fashion of Kurdish women in their country. The old woman paused near the window of the hut, and her face lit up. She kissed her fingertips respectfully and said with satisfaction:

"The sound of the Torah, praised be the Lord, the sound of the Torah!..."

At that moment I felt as though the multiplication tables had also been handed down to us from Mount Sinai.

The total education of the children of Noga was extremely poor: after three or four years of study in the schools of various *ma'abarot,* they were still completely uneducated. Most of them, regardless of age, did not know how to read and write, and they lacked even the most routine study habits.

A well-developed boy of thirteen caused me great difficulty. He refused to come into the classroom and join the class, preferring to stand outside and create a disturbance: he peeped through the windows, knocked on the walls and threw rocks at them. Whenever I tried to call him, he would instantly run away. I could find no net with which to ensnare the wild bird.

One afternoon I was coming home from the village store, which was on the other side of the hill. I was carrying two heavy bags. As I was climbing the hill, the figure of Eliahu suddenly appeared before me. He did not have time enough to run away, as he usually did. I asked him to help me carry the bags home. Eliahu blinked, looked around, and when he made sure there was no one near to see him in his "disgrace", he took the bags from me and brought them to my doorstep. This time I did not permit him to run away. I had a sudden idea. I told him that my door did not close well, and asked him to help me repair it. Eliahu took the hammer from my hand, lifted the door off its hinges easily, made the necessary repair and returned it to its place.

Thus I won Eliahu's heart: I discovered that the lad had "golden hands", and I would regularly find repairs for him to do, all of which he rapidly completed. When we became closer, I discovered that my young friend did not even know how to read the alphabet.

"How is that, Eliahu?" I asked. "In Tiberias, you went to school for three years!..."

"I didn't go, I'd run away. Sometimes I went to take money from the Keren-Hakayemet boxes..."

"Why did you do that?"

"For the movies. Here I've already gotten used to it — there aren't any movies, so it doesn't bother me. But in Tiberias I used to go every day."

I visited Eliahu's home. His father was an old man, tall and almost blind. His mother was an invalid with crippled legs. This did not prevent her from regularly giving birth. Their house was swarming with small children.

I went to the house on a Sabbath. The dirt floor of the hut was covered with a thick layer of shells from sunflower seeds, and chickens pecked comfortably at them. The members of the family were sitting on the beds. On the wall was tacked a giant poster advertising a film; a beautiful screen star clasping her beloved in a passionate kiss...

Eliahu began coming to school as a "listener". He sat with the smaller children, as did Rabbi Akiva in his day, and learned "by ear". In the evenings and on the Sabbath we continued to teach him — I, my husband, my daughter, and any visitor who happened to be in the house. The goal was a hard one: to pierce the wall of ignorance in the soul of a boy who had already despaired of learning, so that he was easily routed by tiny, terrifying letters. Once I lost my patience and raised my voice to him. Eliahu was distressed, and he looked at me with the gaze of a large dog that has been beaten for no fault of its own.

Nevertheless, before the Pesach holiday Eliahu had learned how to read. He then read in class for the first time. The other children were taken aback: why, Eliahu reads "quick as water!"...

His appearance also changed for the better. I was told that his father had hopes that Eliahu would grow up to be a "doctor", and had begun to spoil him: he bought him a shirt and shoes. I once met the father as he was pushing a heavy wheelbarrow loaded with cement blocks. When he saw me, he set the wheelbarrow down, came over to me and waving his fist, cried:

"Beat him! Beat him!"

I was puzzled, and I asked the other workers to ask him what Eliahu had done. They reassured me, explaining that his words were meant to be taken figuratively. This was the accepted formula in Kurdistan. When a child was brought to study the Torah, his parents would say to the teacher: "The flesh is yours, leave me the bones!..."

On the Pesach holiday, Eliahu went to Tiberias for a visit, where his family had formerly lived. He was very excited before the trip, and asked my permission to take the book he had borrowed from the school library with him. Evidently he wanted to "show off" to his friends in Tiberias. I refused permission, which was a mistake.

After the holidays, I noticed that Eliahu had stopped taking books from the library.

"Why don't you take a book to read?"

"I forgot my book in Tiberias..."

"That's very bad," I said. "You've gone against the rule, and you'll have to pay two pounds."

This was a sentence I instantly regretted. The library books had not been bought: most of them had been donated to the library. I suggested a compromise to Eliahu: that he write to Tiberias and ask them to send him the book; or that Eliahu pay his debt by working, so that he could keep on taking out books from the library.

"No!" he refused. "I don't want to read!"

Several days later Eliahu's father, dressed in his tattered work clothes, came into the classroom in the middle of a lesson. He looked worried, and in his hand he held two bills, which he waved in the air.

"You want money? Take it! Let him read at night! At night!"

With the help of an interpreter, I learned the story. In the poor hut, beneath the film poster, Eliahu had begun to read from a book, painfully joining one letter to the next. It was not important what he was reading — it was probably the story of "Ali Baba" or "Cinderella" — but his father, who all his life, had stood in the synagogue shamed by men who could read from the Torah, listened to his halting reading as though it was the speech of the living God. The shame of generations was being rolled away.

When we moved to the village centre of Nehora and the regional school opened there, I found I was sorry to part from Noga. However, the staff of teachers paid regular visits to the villages, to attend parents' meetings and to visit the homes of the settlers. The children awaited these visits impatiently, and took strict care that the visits were equally distributed, and that there was no favouritism.

On one of our visits to Noga, rain began to fall. It was already after sundown. As I was having difficulty in walking, I decided to make only one visit, to a pupil who had been absent for several lessons, in order to find out the reason for his absence. A group of girls from my class surrounded me and almost tore me to pieces. Each of them clamoured for me to visit her. My reply did not satisfy them, and they indignantly turned their backs on me. From a distance I heard them still complaining about me.

On my way back, I met Eliahu. He was standing in the dark beside the gate of his yard, chewing sunflower seeds and awaiting the arrival of the teachers. When he recognized me, he greeted me happily and invited me to come in. I told him about the girls' annoyance and added:

"If I were the mother of one of them, wouldn't they think that at such a late hour an old woman like me ought to go home?"

Eliahu nodded thoughtfully and said, "They don't understand yet, you have to forgive them."

XIII

"ANA KURDI"

"Ana Kurdi" — 'I'm a Kurd' — to Israelis, this is an expression for someone who "doesn't know any tricks", or who pretends to be simple. The immigrants from Kurdistan are regarded as a backward and primitive group, hard to assimilate. This has given them a feeling of inferiority, and Kurdish immigrants are ashamed of being called 'Kurd'. Kurdistan is a large region lying partially in Iraq, partially in Iran, and in places extending into Turkey and the Soviet Union. Immigrants who come from different parts of Kurdistan speak different dialects. The one thing they have in common is that almost all of them have come from small villages or towns, rather than cities. As they lived among Arabs in certain areas, many of them are also accustomed to bearing arms.

This community has brought to the country a smaller number of educated men than any other group of immigrants, and the greatest number of illiterates. At times this creates special problems in school, for the tenth generation of illiterates is often a diametrically opposed parallel to the tenth generation of pupils of 'wise men'.

It is hard for us to imagine what complexes are created in an intelligent, mature man when he cannot under any circumstances grasp even the simplest principles of arithmetic. Those of us who think they were born knowing the multiplication tables owe a debt of gratitude to their parents and teachers for instilling in them the basic elements of culture, without which a man in our times is badly handicapped in making his way in life and in society.

I taught one of the settlers of Noga, the father of five small children, to sign his name. This man, who could swing a heavy hoe with ease, would become covered with sweat as he drew the tiny letters, and the slender pencil would tremble in his courageous hand. After several days, he knew how to write his name legibly. He then approached me with a modest request, one he had evidently had his heart set on for some time:

"I want you to teach me how to sign with a little tail."

The curly signatures he had seen while waiting in various offices and watching the clerks in awe as they signed their names on official papers had apparently found favor in his eyes.

The first task that fell to our lot in Noga was reconciling a man and his wife. We were horrified at the sight of the man beating his young, beautiful wife for no good reason. We were certain that the family was fated to disintegrate. However, we quickly learned that the couple loved one another and that their family life was not in the least shaken by the incident. We had not taken into consideration the customs of the society in which this couple had grown up and been educated.

We learned that where there is love in a family — and it exists among Eastern families just as it does among any other kind — it brightens even the hardest life.

Kadusi was one of the settlers of Noga, a father of five children. Once, during a wedding celebration, the men of the village, who were 'merry with wine,' mocked him: "He dances with his wife in a potato field!"... This surprising information made me curious, and I asked Kadusi about it. At first he was embarrassed and tried to dismiss the subject, but finally he told me about it:

"It's hard for the wife, she work too much. At home she finish with the children, the laundry, the chickens, and she come to the field to help me. And how to make her happy? We finish a row, I take her by the hand and we sing a little."

I once had to send a message to Kadusi to come see me at school about his six-year-old son. For some unknown reason, the little boy refused to enter the classroom of the first grade. He would arrive every morning carrying his satchel, but he would sit down outside beside the wall, wait patiently for four hours till the school day ended, and then go home together with the rest of the children. This state of affairs continued for several weeks after school had begun. The boy hadn't quarrelled with his friends, and he seemed to be an intelligent child. Apparently he had some inner inhibition, but not one of us had succeeded in discovering the reason for his behaviour.

Kadusi came to the school together with his son. When I told him what was the matter, he addressed his son in Arabic and asked him why he wouldn't go into the classroom. The boy raised loving eyes to his father, and after several intimate whispers between the two, I learned from Kadusi that the little boy missed his elder brother, who was in second grade. For that reason, he came to school with his brother every day, waited patiently for the bell at lunchtime, and then walked back with his brother. I had been told that in Kadusi's home, no hand was raised to a child as punishment.

We agreed between us that the older son would return to first grade for a few days, together with his younger brother, until the little one got over his shyness. To my delight, our aim was accomplished in less time than we had expected, and the little boy took his place in the class. I shall not forget the conversation between the father and his little son, carried on lovingly and with a delicacy unusual in these surroundings, where the father's rule over his household is often close to tyranny. During this conversation, I kept thinking of the dance in the middle of the fields...

Illiteracy among the settlers of Noga, and especially among the women — almost all of them — was an almost insoluble problem. It was not easy to convince a young woman, a mother and a housewife whose house was orderly and who cooked on a gas stove and knew how to use an electric iron and a refrigerator, that her main lack now was not — as she thought — a washing machine, but knowing how to read and write.

"I don't have time for lessons, my *children* are learning a lot."

"How do you know they're learning 'a lot'? If you'll study too, they'll have more respect for you, and they won't be ashamed of you in front of their friends whose mothers are educated."

"They won't be ashamed of me! I speak Hebrew, understand every single thing..."

"You only hear the words, you don't 'see' them. You need an 'eye operation'."

"I've got good eyes, don't need any operation!..."

The first winter, there was an upsetting incident in Noga: the woman instructor opened the clothing storehouse to distribute an allotment of winter clothes. She was a young woman, lacking in experience, and she went about the task without taking into consideration the local conditions and the kind of people with whom she was dealing. And, indeed, passions were ignited. The settlers who came to the storehouse did not wait in line, but pushed their way in and grabbed whatever they could lay their hands on from the shelves, without permission. The young woman barely managed to get them to sign for the total value of the things they had taken. After only fifteen families had received clothing the storehouse was emptied, while most of the families had not received the allotment to which they were entitled.

The young instructor came to the team of village workers in tears. An urgent meeting of all the settlers was called at once, and a decision was taken to increase by ten times the sum that every family which had taken things from the storehouse had obligated itself to pay. Whoever objected to the revised estimate might return the things to the storehouse, and then there would be a fair, organized distribution.

The young woman asked. "And what will happen to those who don't return the things?"

One of the elders replied in an offended tone, "Why, we have a synagogue! If we threaten a *kherem* (a ban), everyone will return the things..."

And, indeed, they did, Even the aggressive householder who had been the first to push his way in and make sure of his share of the clothing supply returned every single thing. He was highly incensed by the decision of the village meeting and made a formal vow "on the Torah" that he would never again participate in a meeting of this village.

He did not abide by his resolution, however. Some time later, the village was again in an uproar over the allotment of houses and the right of workers in public services to use the empty houses in the village. A general meeting was again called, and the appearance of the man who had made the vow astonished everyone. The tall man, dressed in a long gown after the custom of his country, stood in the doorway with an angry countenance. In one hand he held a *sidur* (a prayer book), and in the other — a towel. He motioned to one of the elders who was regarded in Noga as an authority on the Torah; the old man rose and went to him and wrapped the towel around the man's neck, leaving the ends untied. Then he opened the *sidur* at the section on "release from vows', and in the silence that reigned in the hall he read these verses: "There is here neither vow nor oath nor abstention nor prohibition nor sanction nor ban nor anathema nor curse, but there is pardon and absolution and condonement. And as the court on earth grant quittance, so doth the court in heaven grant quittance."

After these words the old man, who was very short, rose on tiptoe and tightened the towel around the neck of the sinner who was breaking his vow, and who consequently deserved execution according to the four legal means, of which strangulation is one. The eyes of the poor man almost popped from their sockets, but this went on only a few moments. The garrotting towel was removed, and the recanting sinner recovered. He kissed the hand of his benefactor, and — as he was now released from his vow — raised his voice in complaint:

"Why are there so many Ashkenazim here, eating and drinking at our expense? Anybody who can't find work in Tel Aviv — they send him here to us!..."

And so on, in that vein.

Today we know far less about the 'absorption of immigration' than we did five years ago, on the day we settled in Lachish. Then we were filled with self-confidence, and as soon as the first settlers arrived in Noga, Mordecai hastened to set up an elected committee to manage the affairs of the village, as he had done in the first days of Kfar Achim, or of Arugot, a village of Rumanian immigrants in the neighbourhood of Beer Tuvia.

This turned into a lengthy affair of changing "committees" every second day, for generally a crisis would occur during the first meeting of the elected committee. The people were incapable of grasping the system, and could not understand that the decision of the majority also obligates the minority, even though the minority may be opposed to the decision...

Once I paid a visit to one of the most respected members of the community. I congratulated him on his election to the new committee, to which his son had also been elected. The old man replied:

"Nothing will come of it! They'll all be 'important', and how can one village exist with nine 'heads'?" In explanation of his "viewpoint", he told me a fable: "Once the prophet Eliahu, of blessed memory, went out to wander through the land, and he was joined by a chance traveller. When night approached, the two began to seek shelter, and they knocked at the door of a large house. Within the house, ten brothers were sitting around a huge table laden with every kind of good food. But the brothers drove the guests away, and bolted the door behind them. The prophet Eliahu pronounced a blessing upon them: that they might all be 'important men'.

"Afterwards the two knocked at the door of a poor hut. Its owner welcomed them hospitably, fed them with what he had, and offered them a place to sleep. At midnight Eliahu awakened, rose, went secretly to the barn and slaughtered the poor man's only cow. Then he left the hut.

"Before he parted from the prophet, his companion asked Eliahu to explain his strange behaviour: why had he blessed the wicked men and done wrong to the righteous one?

"Eliahu, of blessed memory, said to him: 'When we were at the house of the righteous man, I saw the Angel of Death standing behind him with a naked sword: a sign that he would not live until daylight. Therefore I slaughtered the cow in his place, and redeemed him.

"'And what could I do to the wicked ones, when they all sat around the same table, the eldest brother at the head, and all the rest obey him? But if *all* of them become 'important', they are lost! One will ask the other for a little water to drink, and his brother will reply, "I am not your servant, I am just as 'important' as you!" And in this way each man will turn against his brother, and they will slaughter one another!'..."

How could we convince the people that paying taxes on

time was the duty of everyone, and that the village itself should mete out punishment to those who neglected to pay? More than once fields of vegetables or cotton — the fruits of constant heavy labour and the work of months — were destroyed by drought, solely because two or three members of the village did not pay their water bills: thereby causing 'Mekorot', the water company, to cut off the water supply of the entire village. The people who suffered the damage turned their wrath on the authorities, and were unable to grasp the connection with paying rates; though in the same village the people willingly give donations to the synagogue, pay well for '*aliyah la'Torah*', and give munificent presents at weddings .The synagogue has an elected committee, which is both responsible and respected by all.

One day one of the men from Noga, an elderly man with a large family of his own, encountered a strange young girl standing in the street in the town of Migdal and crying bitterly. In reply to his questioning, the girl told him that she had come from one of the villages in the Negev to buy clothes for her wedding, but here she had lost her purse with the IL 150 she had saved from her work, and now she was afraid to go home for fear of the punishment awaiting her at the hands of her parents.

The man inquired no further; he took the girl onto his wagon, returned to Noga with her, and went from house to house collecting money until he had collected the required sum. Afterwards he took the girl back to town to buy her trousseau.

In the beginning, it seemed that the settlers of Noga were absolutely incapable of forming themselves into an organized, selfsupporting society. There were endless disputes and disturbances within the village, all springing from the friction between the groups from different countries, or different regions.

At first we thought that the groups differed one from the other only in their difference of origin, Iraqi Kurdistan or Iranian (Persian) Kurdistan. Later we learned that they themselves recognize a third group, the Brazanim, so-called after the name of their city of origin, a city in the Iraqi section of Kurdistan. At times the disputes became so complicated that it seemed to us that not even King Solomon could have succeeded in unravelling the involved reasons for a quarrel and making peace among the rival '*khamulot*' (clans).

During the village's second year, such a severe dispute broke out that the authorities almost despaired. Forty of the villagers went out to the highway and prevented the instructors from entering the village. They blocked the roads to keep out vehicles of the Agency workers, and even refused to allow the regional workers who lived in Noga and worked in other settlements to leave the village and go to their places of work. On the clubhouse, which served as headquarters for the 'rebellion', a huge sign was posted, bearing this inscription:

> **HUNGER STRIKE**
> We want the settlers back to their jobs!
> Don't want the team of instructors back!
> Justice and Peace!

Among those participating in the fast were representatives of all three rival clans, and it was absolutely impossible to find out the precise nature of their grievance, or to clarify with any degree of certainty exactly to *whom* the instructors were supposed to be 'giving *proteksia*' (showing favouritism), the ostensible reason for the strike.

As usual, the newspapers did not pass up the opportunity for a good story, and they made a great deal of the affair. They photographed the strikers and their leaders, the exotic-looking villagers and the sign. They even photographed the herd of sheep, which remained outside the dispute, despite the fact that its ownership was in the hands of all three rivals. In the photograph the herd looks completely united, all the sheep going out to pasture, one beside the other, and led by one shepherd...

The dispute seemed so serious that the Agency was prepared to disband the village and effect an exchange of population: to our joy, matters did not reach that point. Only four families left Noga; and later on, they themselves regretted their step.

That year the area under cultivation in the region that had been untilled for so many generations was doubled. There are no farmers like those of Noga — the only village in the Lachish region that is outstanding for its excellent crop yields, its trees, and its vineyards, the first in the area to bear fruit. It was also the first village to be released from the authority of 'Metakh', the farming and marketing organization of the Agency, which employed the settlers as hired labourers during the first period of settlement. The farms were turned over to the members of Noga earlier than had been planned.

In the winter months, however, when work slacks and the people are indoors much of the time, a variety of problems arise. I have noticed that most disputes break out on the Sabbath, when the village is left without instructors.

This past winter again we received an urgent alarm on a Sabbath morning: "The people in Noga are killing each other!"

As the safeguarding of life outweighs the sanctity of the Sabbath, we got into the pickup truck and in a matter of minutes arrived at the scene of the struggle. The two rival camps were drawn up facing one another, with a distance of about thirty metres between them. The entire village was present. The children were also contributing their share to the general confusion. The width of the street separating the two camps was paved with the rocks thrown by both sides. Eighteen casualties had already been removed from the battlefield. Mordecai and I separated at once, each going to a different camp. I ran to a girl who was wounded, blood still streaming from an open wound on her head. Her face was so swollen it was almost unrecognizable. The nurse was standing beside the wounded girl pleading with her to go into the house and let the nurse bandage her head; but the Kurdish girl, filled with the spirit of battle, stood firm and refused to abandon her post:

"Let the police see me like this! I'll show them!"

I managed, with some difficulty, to collect the schoolchildren and remove them from the field of battle. The children followed me unwillingly, as though they were being unjustly dragged away by some tyrant...

Twenty of the firebrands were arrested on that Sabbath, and said the blessing for *havdala* behind the bars of the jail in the police station. Yet even this bloody clash did not leave its mark for long. At a wedding held in Noga a short time after the incident the rivals all made peace and again fraternized with one another, brothers dwelling together. The wedding celebration continued, according to custom, for a week, moving from house to house. Relatives and village dignitaries were honoured with a visit. The entire celebrating crowd would then move to their house and there they would begin all over again. Tired and happy, the bride and groom marched at the head of the procession to the strains of flute and drum, while three generations — the grandmother, mother, and sister of the groom — danced before them with ancient oriental charm.

Indeed, many were the "rejoicings" in Noga! A *brit-milah* for the newborn son is a great holiday in the village, as are engagements and weddings. The Kurds think nothing of the expense of a celebration of this kind. This community has the experience of generations, experience that has taught them that the expense is worthwhile in the long run; for the blessing to the entire community, in the mutual affection and strengthening of group ties created by such a celebration, is priceless.

The young people mature rapidly and marry at an early age. Acceptable subjects for neighbourly discussion are: 'Whose turn is coming up? Who is well thought of, and what are the conditions? How was the wedding?' For a magnificent, beautiful wedding is a deep experience for both the individual and the group, one that is remembered by everyone for years afterward.

The younger generation is striving to become assimilated into the life of the country as a whole, to adapt themselves quickly to new ways and new concepts, to adopt the ordinary Israeli mode of dress, to furnish their homes in "modern" style, to sing and dance exactly like the 'sabras' — without realizing that we, too — the long-time settlers and native Israelis — borrowed and drew our songs from various sources, and not always desirable ones.

At one of the first weddings in Noga the settlers danced the "Tchopi" — a traditional Kurdish dance, in which the women as well as the men participate. For hours the closely-pressed bodies move in a long, waving line, and at the head of the swaying column dances the minstrel, waving his brightly-coloured kerchief and making jests in honour of the lovers and in honour of the guests at the celebration.

The youth instructor sat beside me and watched the slow, deliberate dance with impatience. Finally he exclaimed: "I've got to show them how to dance!"

He jumped up from his place, took the young people out of the line of dancers and together with them started a wild *hora*. Their feet kicked up clouds of dust from the unpacked earth of the yard, and they gave deafening screams: "Oh-ya! Yo-yah! A-ba! I-ma! Mi anakhnu? Mi kamonu?"

I can unashamedly admit that in my eyes as well, they looked like savages.

At the same celebration I suggested to my daughter and the young teachers who had come to the wedding that they try to learn the "Tchopi". It is not a difficult dance to learn, and after a short time they too weaved slowly in the close-packed line of dancers. The old women enjoyed the sight, and one of them gave me a compliment:

"Your daughter's not a 'Hungaria' at all! She's like us, a Kurd!"

"ANA KURDI"

The poet, Y.D. Kamson, was visiting in Nehora when the rabbi from Noga came to our house for a Sabbath visit. As was the custom, the rabbi did not come alone; to do so would have been beneath his dignity. He was accompanied by three members of his community. The poet was deeply impressed by their appearance, which most certainly did not remind him of the rabbis of his native Lithuania. Here are some lines of his description, from his poem, "*Sabbath in Nehora*":

> ... From Noga to Nehora, on the Sabbath day
> To the council head, to Mordecai
> Came the rabbi, and of the men of Babylon, three:
> Strong as Shishai, Ahiman and Talmai.

When I look at the people of Noga, with their charm and their health of spirit, their endurance and their love of work, their love of the land and the purity of their family lives; their poverty and their secret envy of us, the "learned ones", whose attainments they cannot emulate; their simplicity and their susceptibility to erupt in violence at the urging of their quick passions — I hear in my heart, a 'hymn of praise for the peoples of all lands.'

XIV

A "BIGAMOUS" WEDDING

THE RABBI of Noga — or, as he was termed in the village, their *Khacham* ('wise man') — had many worries with his flock. The youth had changed almost beyond recognition. The young people would play football and hold bicycle races on the highway on the Sabbath. They had all become boastful and ill-mannered. They were no longer dependent on their parents. They all earned money, and sometimes a father had to apply to his son for charity, like a beggar. They told the "wise man" that at the films to which the young people flocked, abandoned women were exhibited on the wall. Once the *Khacham* was riding with his son in a bus, and when the son opened his wallet to pay for the tickets, he revealed a series of photographs of young beauties, naked as Eve, in the celluloid pockets of the wallet. The father could not control himself, and he reprimanded his son.

The son replied rudely: "That's the way things are now. Everybody behaves the way he wants to, and why not?"

And if the *Khacham* himself has lost control of his household, what could the heads of the other households say? Each of them pretended that in *his* household "everything was all right", but their hearts were fearful for their sons, and even more — for their daughters. The daughters began to refuse to get married at a suitable age, when they were still tender and biddable. Even the sons rebelled sometimes, choosing to go into the army rather than to marry at an early age, be exempted from army service, and devote themselves to their farms.

In the house of one of the settlers, which was very crowded, there was a young girl who had just immigrated to the country.

In her childhood she had been engaged to the son of the family, in their country of origin. Her parents had recently agreed to send her to the house of her fiancé by herself, despite the dangers and difficulties, for the time had come for the wedding. And the young man? He announced that he didn't want her at all, he was only a little boy when his parents had made the engagement, but now he wanted to choose a girl that he liked, by himself... Oh, what disgrace his shameless behaviour had brought upon his family!

The greatest concern of the *Khacham* was one of the three companions who frequently accompanied him; these three formed a kind of unofficial escort during all his walks and visits. All three were tall and strong — the three the poet compared to Shishai, Ahiman, and Talmai. One was a relative of the *Khacham* himself, and his childhood friend. For years this man had been married to a quiet, hardworking woman, but she had evil luck with her children. Although she bore children — almost every year — sooner or later they all died of illness. What had this couple not done against the evil eye, against djinns, against the hidden powers of evil! The father of the *khacham* had also written charms for the poor woman, and had given her amulets. She had even taken her children to the Moslem "*yadonim*", but nothing had helped. The woman grew white-haired before her time, and began to dye her hair with "*khina*" (henna).

Only little Moshe, her youngest child, was still living. She would not cut his hair, for she had vowed to burn it on the grave of Rabbi Shimon Bar Yochai when she reached Eretz-Israel. Jars of oil were bought to feed the sacred fire, and much money was distributed to the poor. And, indeed, she fulfilled her vow and Moshe grew up in Eretz-Israel, and he entered school, to study the Torah. Some time passed before the mother would agree to the teacher's demands that she remove some of the "medals" and "hands" that were hung around his neck and sewn into all his clothing — not all of them, of course, to be on the safe side.

Once the nurse met the mother and her son in the street. She patted the child's cheek, and said, "Here, you see — he's healthy even without all the junk you used to hang on him. And where have all the 'demons' gone?"

The mother gave a happy laugh. "There aren't any demons in Eretz-Israel. Here, blessed be the Name, there's electricity."

Suddenly things changed. At the beginning of winter, Moshe caught a cold. Even after he was up and around again and had returned to school, he complained constantly of pain, and would lie in bed as much as he could, peculiar behaviour in a child.

The nurse and the doctor noticed the child's condition, and they began taking his temperature morning and evening. Finally they sent him to the hospital in Jerusalem for examination. Word came from there that little Moshe was suffering from leukemia, and there was no hope for him.

Fate, which had once smiled on the miserable parents, had turned against them again. The child himself showed no signs of his disease in his external appearance, except that he became very spoiled and dominated the entire household. From time to time the doctor would send him to the hospital for several weeks, and there they requested blood donations for the child. Everyone knew that the "Ashkenazim" give blood without thinking about it twice, as though they aren't Jews at all. It is written in the Torah that the blood is the soul — and who invented such a cruel and heathenish practice: to drain the blood of a living man for the sake of a sick one? However, as he had no choice, the father paid the full price and bought blood from the hospital's regular donors. The mother refused even to entertain the idea that her son's life was in danger. Why, he was already big and strong, and he studied the Torah — and children just didn't die in Israel...

The child's condition grew more serious, and his appearance changed for the worse. Again the parents began to seek amulets and appeal to sorcerers.

The father grew gaunt — he became a shadow of his former self, as though he himself were ill. More than once he was seen wandering around intoxicated, and in the course of time he began to absent himself from the village at frequent intervals; the work on his farm was done haphazardly, by hired labourers. The rumour spread that he was making trips to the city for the purpose of making a match with a girl who was young, though crippled. Apparently he had decided that the time had come for him to concern himself with the problem of leaving a *"kaddish"* on earth, lest he be left with no hope of the next world. In the old country, men took two wives, or even three, especially when the first wife grew too old to bear children. Then the husband would take an additional wife, to bear more children and to help with the housework.

The mother, gripped by a growing fear for the fate of her child, paid no heed to her husband's frequent absences until one of her pitying neighbours brought the rumour to the "poor woman":

"*Ya khabibti,* to a man we are like dogs. If we don't have children, he drives us from the house. If he won't give you food, or if he beats you so that you will grant him a divorce — what will you do? He must have a *"kaddish"*, it is a commandment for him, and you — what can you do to him?"

Now the mother attacked like a wounded lioness. She quickly dressed in her best garments and all her many ornaments, asked her neighbour to watch her child until her return, and left the house like a whirlwind. And thus she appeared before the woman instructor:

"Look, instructor, we believe everything you say, and all you do is tell lies. You said that in Eretz-Israel children don't die — then let them not die! You said that in Eretz-Israel men don't take second wives while they've got a wife living — so is it that here they force you to give a divorce? You have to find me a great doctor who'll give me a medicine so I myself can bear another child. I must bear one more child, so my husband and I will have a *"kaddish"*, so we won't burn in the flames of Gehennom when we die. You've got to take care of this, — what else are you here for? Why don't you say something?"

The same day, the child was again taken to the hospital in Jerusalem. The nurse and the woman instructor who came to take him filled his hands with sweets and gave him a book with coloured pictures. The mother, too, travelled to Jerusalem together with her son, to stay there with relatives, so she might visit her sick son in the hospital every day.

The doctor told her, "It's best that you not be too far away..."

On the evening of the same day, the father danced at the wedding of one of the young men of the village. It was a lovely wedding, and many guests came from outside the village. The "orchestra" — a flute and a drum — played the prolonged, exciting melodies that have been a tradition for so many generations. At first only the older people danced, while the young girls in their short, puffed modern dresses stood to one side. But the melody and the rhythm gave them no rest, and in the end they, too, joined the circle. Everyone danced, but the father of the sick little Moshe danced more than anyone else. He stood at the head of the line of dancers, waving his kerchief, tall and active, as though he himself were the man in whose honour the celebration was being held.

The woman instructor noticed that the *Kackham's* eyes did not leave his dancing friend. She could not contain herself, and she addressed the *Khacham* in a sympathetic voice: "Honoured rabbi, how can a man behave like that? His son may even be dead already, at this very minute!"

The *Khacham* replied, "To rejoice is one of the greatest of good deeds. Rejoicing that is commanded by the Torah outweighs death."

The rumour was verified: the man had, indeed, become betrothed to a young woman, and intended to bring her into his household, in addition to his first wife. The responsible village authorities decided to adopt an attitude of caution and courtesy regarding the internal affairs of family and community, even when they led to disputes — and not to lay down a set of moral rules according to their own personal views. As to bigamy — they decided to leave that question to be settled by the laws of the state, which punish with imprisonment both the man who breaks them, and the man who performs the ceremony (without which, incidentally, a man of this 'backward' community would not touch a woman). Everyone knows that the guardians of the law watch vigilantly, and that a man cannot legally undergo a second marriage ceremony without first divorcing his first wife.

And behold, all the members of the village received a traditional wedding invitation, printed in letters of gold, with a picture of two doves billing, and above them the letters *Bet-Heh* (an abbreviation for 'By the grace of God'). The parents of the bride and bridegroom (the bridegroom, sadly, was orphaned of his father, and only his mother gave the invitation) invited the members of the village to the wedding celebration of their children.

Perhaps an unconscious desire to find a kind of Avishag to warm the chilled blood of old age in his veins was working on the pious husband? Only the Lord knows what is in a man's heart. The bridegroom had not understood the advice of the lawyer whom he had consulted, and who had counselled him to announce publicly that he was bringing a "maid" into his house. The lawyer explained to him that among the Ashkenazim, it was not unusual for a husband to be unfaithful to his wife, and it happened even in the best families. In his innocence, the bridegroom did not understand why it should be forbidden him to bring home the "maid" with cymbals and dancing, — and at this opportunity, to hold a feast for hundreds of people.

He appeared in the office of the Area Council with a request to hire the bus in order to transport the bride and her large family. His thick beard, which had been carefully tended for several decades, was no longer in evidence. His face was shaven smooth as silk, an unavoidable necessity.

In the Council office, of course, they spoke to him strictly, and warned him that he might well spend his wedding night, after the marriage ceremony, in prison, on the charge of bigamy.

However, the man was firm in his decision, like a man who is convinced that the right is on his side: "I have invited five hundred people to the wedding. I am not doing anything underhand. I have no future without a son, and I have a document about it."

The "document" he showed had been given him by the gynecological department of a hospital, and it stated, black on white, that the man's first wife had been examined by doctors and found to be beyond the age of childbearing.

The social worker was called in, and he paid a visit to the man's first wife, who had meanwhile moved into a new asbestos hut that had been built for her in the yard. The old furniture had been moved there from the house, which had been furnished anew. The woman seemed to have accepted her fate, and she said:

"What can you do, he's already bought new chairs..."

To the great astonishment of the social worker and the instructors, it was clearly apparent that the entire village stood behind the man. And what could you learn from their talk? According to the laws of the state, a man who wanted to marry a second time first had to divorce his first wife, and make financial arrangements for her support. But what can be done when neither the woman herself, nor her family, regard a financial settlement as a just solution? The very thought that for the price of compensation it is permissible for a man to send away an aging woman, the victim of fate, who has been his chief helpmeet, to thrust her out of his life like an unwanted possession — the very thought causes a shudder and a heartfelt feeling of opposition among all the members of the community, including the crippled girl from the poor quarter of the great city, with whom the match had been made. Why should she drive out the mistress of the house, and perhaps by doing so, shorten her life? Would it not be even harder for them to support the older woman separately till the end of her days, as they were bound to do, lest it be said: 'You have inherited from her, and you have driven her out?'

The magnificent white bridal dress which, as was customary, was rented from the store for the wedding ceremony alone, never in its days served at a wedding so strange and sad. Hundreds of guests sat around the tables, among them the bridegroom's first wife as well, but the orchestra from the neighbouring village, famous in the area, which would make the crowd merry at every wedding, was absent this time. A tragedy had occurred in the neighbouring village, whose members were from the same community: one of the daughters of the village, an unmarried woman who had reached the age of thirty without being asked for in marriage, had drowned herself. The entire village was in mourning — approving, by its demonstration of sympathy, the act of the young woman; she had sought an honourable way out of a life of single loneliness, which the community regarded as a shameful position for a woman, and a disgrace to her family.

The veil glistened on the head of the bride. She had been lucky, she had found an honourable solution in time; she was saved from the unbearable situation in which she might have remained: superfluous, purposeless, and alone in a cold, strange world. Why, therefore, should she hate the older woman who had consented to accept her?

At the end of the celebration, their close relations escorted the married couple, according to custom, to the doorway of their house, where they were startled by the words of the bridegroom, who grasped his bride's hand and declared:

"God in heaven sees my heart: I am guiltless! This fate, too, has been decreed from on high, and I must bear it."

XV

HELPING HANDS

When we first moved to Lachish, we felt like explorers in a strange land. Friends who came to our aid were a great comfort to us, and strangers became friends through offering their help to the project.

"*Great are the needs of Thy people.*" When you have come from a well-established settlement where life goes on in its set routine and the municipal services seem to be carried out of themselves, moving to a new settlement makes you feel as though the ground has been jerked from under your feet: the electricity goes out, the radio falls silent, the house shrinks to one room, the highway seems to disappear, and with every step, the foot sinks into mud. The most ordinary foods cannot be obtained, and when they are obtained by great effort, they cannot be kept without ice in a house that is not cool. And then there is the constraint that overcomes one when darkness falls.

The new immigrants themselves had problems that were far more difficult: numerous children, diseases to which all were susceptible during the first period, loneliness, lack of a clear vision of the ultimate goal, and a lack of faith that the goal would ever be attained. There were also plagues unmentioned in the Bible such as our plague of hornets. Formerly, the hornets had held undisputed ownership of the wild fields. For years they had ruled this area, until suddenly they were disturbed by the activities of the new creatures who invaded their territory. The children went around with swollen eyes or swollen cheeks. Once, when passing one of the huts, I heard a child screaming at the top of his lungs. I entered the hut and saw the horrified mother, surrounded by little children. One of them was lying on the floor, writhing with pain: a hornet had stung him in the tenderest of spots...

The problems fell upon us all at once — security, employment, housing, health, education — and every one of them required an instant solution. We would turn from one matter to another, unable to devote ourselves wholly to any one aim. But from time to time some modest volunteer would appear and ease our task with his devoted service.

Before we left Kfar Warburg, a tall woman with silver hair and a noble countenance appeared on our doorstep; she informed us that she was placing her services at our disposal for three days a week, on a voluntary and unpaid basis. She added that she was prepared to do anything at all that was assigned to her, even "sponja"! (Scrubbing floors).

From her relatives in Kfar Warburg, we learned that she was a former teacher in the Rehavia High School in Jerusalem. Her husband, the teacher and author Moshe Carmon, had died a short time ago, and she had retired on a pension. In Bet Hakerem she had a beautiful house, surrounded by a grove of pines. Her son was a high-ranking officer in the army; she had grandchildren, and was admired by the entire family. But the name "Lachish" fascinated her, and she decided to devote herself to working with the new immigrants in the Lachish region, as she had done for years in the *ma'abarot* of the Jerusalem area.

We rejoiced over these reinforcements, and Miriam Carmon became our partner in all the experiences of those days. She too received a hut in Noga, near us, and she immediately set to work. She cleaned and scrubbed the old hut until it sparkled, hoed the weeds around the house, brought broken pieces of brick and paved a path to the hut. Then she began to visit the families and seek out pupils she could teach to read and write.

Everything in her hut was bright and pleasant: the curtains, the embroidered tablecloth, the sparkling kerosene lamps, and she herself. This long-time teacher, who had studied under the best teachers of her generation and had herself taught tens of classes of pupils and had instructed many young teachers, had both education and the wisdom of experience. Unusual pupils began to come to her — the dignitaries of the village and committee members who admitted to her that their lack of knowledge of arithmetic disturbed them greatly. She attempted to teach them the secret of these complicated matters. An atmosphere of culture abounded in the tiny hut of this experienced teacher, who revealed a capacity for opening the eyes of the blind. Her pupils "really" learned to read and write: they learned the multiplication tables, they practised writing letters, and some of them simply learned how to sign their names.

Long discussions were carried on in her hut. She was an event in the life of the village; she would get the settlers into discussions about the affairs of the nation, and try to fire them with her own enthusiasm for tilling the soil. She was continually bringing her new friends seedlings or seeds which seemed to her suitable for the soil of the Lachish region.

She won our hearts with her honesty and her courage. We knew that she was in ill health, and that her family had urged her not to further endanger it with this work and with the repeated trips that were exhausting for a person of her age. However, this was the one subject which she would not discuss under any circumstances.

The first winter in Lachish, before the roads and highways were paved, was a hard one. On a rainy, stormy night, when 'the windows of the heavens had been opened', Mordecai went to persuade Miriam to move temporarily to our hut, in order not to leave her alone in utter isolation. The distance between one hut to the next was around a hundred metres, and no guards patrolled our neighbourhood, as it was outside the "settled area" of lower Noga.

Mordecai saw that the wind had broken the window-frame in Miriam's hut and smashed the windowpanes. It was as cold indoors as out. Miriam was pursuing a rat that was making a determined effort to share her hut. Against her will, Mordecai moved her to our house.

We drank coffee and felt sorry for all the people whose jobs obliged them to be outside on a night like this. We decided that it wasn't easy even to be a *'fedayin'* (an infiltrating terrorist). Mordecai told us that the first family of the team of village workers was supposed to have arrived today from Ramat Gan. The man, the new secretary, was a former seaman; he had decided to move to Lachish "with both feet." His wife would be the nurse in Noga. They had one baby, and they intended to be permanent residents here.

At that moment the door opened, and a young woman with a baby in her arms appeared in the doorway. She was soaked with rain, but she gave us a broad smile, showing two rows of white teeth. Despite the pouring rain, the young couple had decided to make the move on the appointed day: they had ordered a truck in advance, and they couldn't afford paying for a truck and not using it; but by the time they had gotten their furniture loaded and started out, the short winter day was almost over. "Lachish", at that time, was *terra incognita,* and the truck driver was not familiar with the roads in our region.

They lost their way, and at nightfall reached Kibbutz Erez, on the border of the Gaza Strip.

We did not learn all this the same evening. The couple apologised for arriving so late, and for the truck driver's refusing to unload their belongings beside their hut, because of the depth of the mud there.

It was almost midnight. The young couple would not agree under any circumstances to spend the night at our house. Miriam, too, wanted to go back to her own hut, but this we refused to allow. However, the young woman quieted us and said that they were prepared to take their baby and spend the night in Miriam Carmon's hut — their blankets had escaped the rain. She went out with the same lovable smile on her lips, and with that she won my heart for ever.

To this day, Menachem and Carmela are our next-door neighbours. As they had no parents, they "adopted" us. After they had been with us for some time, I learned that Carmela was the sole survivor of her family, and had gone through all the horrors of the death camps. In this country she had served in the army, received training as a practical nurse, and had worked for several years in the operating theater of one of the large city hospitals. We were overjoyed when we saw how she worked in our clinic and the way she approached her patients.

Suddenly, half a year later, Carmela informed us, giving no explanation, that she would no longer work for Kupat Kholim. The nurse from Shakhar subsequently told us that during a lecture to the medical personnel in the new immigrant villages, a chief nurse with a highly responsible position in Kupat Kholim had said:

"Nevertheless, I know that a *good* nurse, one who knows her profession, won't go to the Negev..."

Carmela waited to hear no more: she rose from her seat, left the room, and did not return. The administration of Kupat Kholim completely ignored the incident: except for Carmela, no one had protested, and the chief nurse had many prerogatives.

Carmela's decision meant a loss to Kupat Kholim as an organization — and the loss of a good nurse in our village.

I grasped what lay behind Carmela's smile when, during the Sinai Campaign, her husband was sent on a long and secret voyage in a frigate, around the Cape of Good Hope. The Sinai Campaign was short, and the fate of all those who took part in it was known in a matter of days. This was not the case with the crews of two naval ships that were at sea for almost two months; until the actual day of their arrival, we could not be certain that they would safely reach the shores of Eilat.

Carmela remained alone with little Uri. She neither wept nor complained of the strain of that long period of waiting. Every morning I would meet her with the little boy in her arms, and she would give me a smile fresh as a flower. Inwardly, her mind was on the vast expanses of the ocean beyond Africa; and her smile was the expression of her unwavering belief and hope.

Later on, during the most trying days I ever experienced in Lachish, Carmela proved herself a constant and loyal friend. I saw her weep then for the first time — over sorrows not her own.

During our first two months in Noga, members of the Tel Aviv Dental Association paid a visit to the Lachish region, and Mordecai accompanied them as their guide. Suddenly he was embraced by a man whom, at first, he did not recognize.

Two members of the group, Dr. Sussman and his wife, had been among the founders of Kvutzat Schiller, near Rehovot, at the same time Mordecai and I were in the group that was founding Kfar Bilu. We had all been active in the Labour Movement in Rechovot during that era when it was generally assumed that the Jewish people had too large an *inteligentsia,* and many of them attempted to become tillers of the soil.

The Sussmans could not control their excitement at finding

friends of former days in this isolated spot. An aftermath of this meeting was the birth of an excellent and important voluntary project: the Dental Association of Tel Aviv adopted the Lachish region and established a dental clinic in Noga, and later in Nehora. Members of the Association contributed one work-day per month, and they took turns in working in the clinic. The project operated efficiently for over two years, and to this day our old friends are loyal supporters of Lachish.

We found another pair of helpers in the very beginning — a couple named Tamari, from the United States. Both were long-time Zionists, who had sold their business in America and retired, settling in Ashkelon to spend the remainder of their days in the country to which they had devoted so much love and effort throughout their lives. They lived in Ashkelon, and they came to Noga in their car almost every day. There was no work which they looked down on, or thought beneath their dignity. The elderly man repaired and catalogued the first used books the village received as a gift. This was the beginning of our library. I begged another gift from the editorial staff of *Davar* — rolls of newsprint; and Mr. Tamari cut the rolls of paper into drawing tablets that provided a supply for the school for two whole years.

His wife, Rose, helped make clothes for the children. She sewed and fitted curtains for the school, and for all the public offices. In addition, their car was almost always at our disposal, for they both knew how to drive.

One afternoon the two arrived, and agreed to spend the night with us. The husband stayed to help Mordecai, and Rose took me to the agricultural school of "Kanot" in their car, to bring the first seedlings to be planted in the first agricultural school of the Lachish region. I was impatient. For dozens of years I had not seen such an utterly barren landscape. Therefore I urged action — plant seedlings!

When the workers in the "Kanot" nursery discovered for whom their seedlings were destined, they gave us 'special treatment' — they filled the trunk of the car to overflowing with potted seedlings. Every few minutes another of the nursery workers would come running with an additional present: "This ought to do well in your soil, too!" How could we possibly refuse?

We left at sundown, despite the army's strict prohibition against travelling on the roads of Lachish after sundown. We were only two women, and we were a little afraid. When we came to the crossroads of the Sa'ad road, Rose told me that something was wrong with the car. I also smelled something burning. Suddenly we heard a loud crack. The car fell to one side and stopped on the spot. From the weight of all the pots, the back axle had broken. It was beyond repair, and we were still only halfway to our destination.

In the dark, in danger, and on foot, we reached Metsudat Yoav — the former police station of Iraq-Suidan. By order of the commanding officer, we were sent home with a military escort, in a manner worthy of distinguished citizens. We found our respective husbands already lamenting our fate.

When the village centre of Nehora was set up and we moved there from Noga, additional volunteers appeared, whose work was of the greatest value. The first was Serakh Danin-Yanai, daughter of an old and well-known family. When Rivka Alper's book, *"The History of One Family"*, appeared, a reception was held in the family's honour at the home of the President. All the members of this many-branched family were present at the reception. In this family, Sephardim have intermarried with Ashkenazim over four generations. Among the speakers that evening, Serakh made an especially vivid impression:

"Everyone talks about the mingling of communities, and I consider myself a direct result of that mingling. It is as though two influences are at work within me: at times the father's is the stronger, and at times — the mother's."

This was the gist of her words, and the guests were enchanted by her picturesque analysis when she described the things for which she loved the Sephardim, and those for which she loved the Ashkenazim.

More should be told about this "result", Serakh, who was raised in a household which emphasized moral values and placed the value of working for the general welfare of one's society above anything else. She was educated in the first school for girls in Jaffa, when it was still battling for Hebrew as the language of instruction. Serakh chose teaching as her profession. At first she worked in Rishon le'Tsion, later in the Caucasian quarter of Tel Aviv, for she was drawn to the children of poor neighbourhoods. Her pedagogic ability gained rapid recognition, and for years she gave classes in instruction to teachers of elementary grades.

When I was assigned the task of setting up the first school in the region (today the Shimoni School, in Nehora), I consulted Serakh about my fears that I would be unable to create an atmosphere of interest in study in a school for children of new immigrants. The teachers were all inexperienced, as I was myself. Four years had passed since my teaching days in the Qastina *ma'abara*. Today the requirements for directing an educational institution were greater. Who would give demonstration lessons to the teachers, who would examine the work of these beginners? The supervisors of the Department of Education were already overburdened with their duties, and they were unable to devote special attention to one school.

Serakh volunteered her services on condition that the authorities in the Department of Education would not regard it as a duplication of their work. This condition was fulfilled, and she took upon herself the responsibility for guidance of the teachers, especially those who taught the lower grades. She did this on a voluntary basis as her contribution to the building of Lachish.

During a period of three years, Serakh spent one full day per month in our school. This woman, who was known to be in ill health, did not miss a visit in any kind of weather. At a meeting in the evening she would receive a report on the various classes, the successes and the failures. Next morning, with the first bell, she would go to the school, visit the classrooms, and give demonstration lessons. One day each month the teachers would make a trip to see her, to decide on new approaches in their work, and to plan their future programs. When the teachers said: "We're going to see Serakh today", it reminded me of *chassidim* going on a visit to their rebbe "to hear his sacred words..."

Another volunteer beloved by all was Matilda Izarov, who came from South Africa. Her three sons were already married, and all of them had children. All her life Matilda had been attracted to Eretz-Israel, and on this visit she decided to settle in Lachish for a year or two.

She taught handicrafts to the girls and young women, and was a friend to every one of them. This was a rare instance of a courageous woman who willingly lowered her financial and cultural standards in order to help her people, despite the fact that she herself did not yet even know Hebrew. She wanted only to give and to help, and her contribution was welcomed with gratitude and appreciation.

XVI

'WISDOM HATH BUILDED HER HOUSE'

ONE SABBATH, during a *khamsin,* an elderly woman came to visit us. She was panting from the heat, and accompanied by a young woman. This was Rivka Ben-Tolila and her daughter-in-law. She was known to me by report. She was very busy during the week, and she did not travel on the Sabbath; and so she had come on foot. These were her first words:

"They told me that another wise woman has settled in Lachish. I've come to make your acquaintance."

I accepted her words as the highest of compliments, for I had been told by everyone of the wisdom of the woman who stood before me.

She was the mother of the six brothers in the village of Shakhar. It was hard to believe that these six were brothers, for they were born one after the other, year after year, and now the difference in their ages was no longer evident in their appearance. They were all tall and strong, talented and good-humoured. Three of them already had families. The little grandchildren adored their grandmother.

They formed a family 'kibbutz'. A co-operative settlement composed of the Ben-Tolila family in the village of Shakhar in the Lachish region. This family transformed 150 dunams of land that had been uncultivated for generations into a fruitful farm. This is the wealthiest and most productive farm in all the villages of Lachish — despite the fact that its owners came to the country through the Youth Aliyah, and with no capital. When you ask them the secret of their success, the young men give a unanimous reply: "Mother."

Rivka Ben-Tolila herself works harder than anyone else. Among her acquaintances, her tremendous creative energy arouses a certain awe. She needed no instruction in the new conditions of life she found in the country: her origin, the sound education she received at home, and the suffering she experienced during her own lifetime have strengthened her and moulded her into a woman of firm moral character and stability of outlook, whose opinions command respect even among those who disagree with them. To her sons as well, she has given a heritage of culture, work, and a spiritual relationship with her.

All the Biblical verses about "a virtuous woman" might have been written about her. She does not simply cook or sew — she is an artist in the kitchen, as a seamstress, and in every other household craft. It would be hard to find another such industrious pair of hands in combination with such good commonsense and wisdom born of experience. Her strong, active personality resembles that of a soldier who has been under fire many times, and who knows how to defend his position.

Rivka Ben-Tolila was born in Tituan, the capital of Spanish Morocco, which is looked upon as the Jerusalem of North Africa. To this day there is a street in the city of Tituan named after her father, Rabbi Yaakov Ben-Tolila, founder and supervisor of the yeshiva, *Yagdil Torah*.

This famous family has its origins in Toledo, Spain, where it settled prior to the Moslem conquest of 711 A.D. With the expulsion of the Jews from Spain, the family of Ben-Tolila (or Toledo) travelled to Morocco, where members of the family held many distinguished positions.

Rivka Ben-Tolila married Rafael Ben-Tolila, the son of a well-known family of distinguished merchants. Rafael Ben-Tolila expanded his business and moved to Ifni, the southernmost Spanish outpost in Morocco, on the border of the Sahara desert. There he supplied food and clothes to the army. When the Fascist revolution broke out, under the leadership of Franco, the civil war reached even as far as Ifni. Franco's soldiers captured the fortress; with rifle butts, they broke into the house of Ben-Tolila, the sole Jewish family living within the fortified area. Franco's troops were searching for Rafael Ben-Tolila, who had collaborated with the Republicans; but the doorway was blocked by the body of a pregnant woman, to whom were clinging five small children. The Fascists beat her and demanded that she reveal her husband's hiding-place. She remained silent under the blows.

Rivka Ben-Tolila paid great sums of money to the men who were concealing her husband; and when they betrayed him and turned him over to the forces of the new government, she paid bribes to men who promised to effect his release. In the end, the "release" arrived, together with official notification that her husband had been executed for treason.

She was also given her husband's last letter: ... "At the time of writing this, I know what awaits me. Be of good courage, and trust in God, and He will help you. Go back to your father's house, for the children's sake. You have been a loyal wife to me, and I am certain that you will educate the children — including the one whom I shall never know — in the spirit of the traditions of Israel. Do everything in your power for the continued unity of the family, and your sons will be like seedlings of olive trees around your table."

With her small sons, the widow returned to Tituan, the city of her birth, where she remained until the death of her father in 1947. The family then moved to Tangier, and Rivka Ben-Tolila opened a store together with her eldest son, who had meanwhile become a young man and had begun working. Her friends and acquaintances say that many men had honourable intentions towards the virtuous widow, despite the fact that she had six children who were almost grown. When I asked her about this, she shrugged her shoulders: "I loved my husband."

Messengers from Eretz-Israel reached Tangier, and there were also Zionist youth movements in the city. The three older sons joined the Union of Religious Chalutzim, and the three younger sons joined "B'nei-Akiva". The first to immigrate to Israel, in 1951, were Amram and Moshe. A year later, Shmuel, Khalfon, and Rafael (who was born after the death of his father and was named after him) arrived in the country. The eldest, Yaakov, had married, and remained in Tangier with his mother. The brothers went to Kibbutz Yavneh, in the southern part of the country, for agricultural training. When the "second shipment" arrived, the two older brothers were already in the army. A year later two more went into the army. The young Rafi, who was 'bored' with being left alone, went with them as well and volunteered for army service, although he was not yet of conscription age.

The young reporter, Amos Lev, who fell in the Sinai campaign, published a story in *"Ba'makhaneh"* about the five Ben-Tolila brothers, and here is a description of the enlistment of the younger three:

"... When they reached the enlistment office, they stood in line to enlist, one behind the other. The first reported.

"Family name, please?"

"Ben-Tolila."

He was enlisted and moved on. The second reported, and replied to the same question:

"Ben-Tolila."

The clerk glanced at him, smiled, and enlisted him. The third reported, and when he too replied "Ben-Tolila" to the query, the clerk put his pen down and said with some annoyance:

"Listen, young man, stop joking. Now, what's your name?"

"Who's joking?" Rafael replied. "My name's Ben-Tolila, and I'm the brother of the two before me. And if it's not too hard, look in the files and you'll find that a year ago two other Ben-Tolilas enlisted here, and they're our brothers, too."

While they were in Nachal, the brothers received additional agricultural training at one of the kibbutzim in Western Galilee. They dreamed of settling in a new region and establishing a large mixed farm. Suddenly they were informed, in a telegram, that their mother was arriving in Israel, with no prior notification.

In the port of Haifa, people stared at the 'regiment' of soldiers who met a lone, elderly woman with cries of joy, and actually carried her on their shoulders. When they returned to the kibbutz, they found a surprise: their room had been decorated with flowers, and a cake had been baked for them. The next day a party was held in honour of the new arrival.

The mother did not delay: she travelled to Tiberias, bought everything that was necessary, and in their room she also gave a party for all the friends of her sons, and the members of the kibbutz who had prepared her own reception. The sons ate their mother's confections joyously, the sweets they had dreamed of ever since they had separated from her.

Rivka Ben-Tolila made a speech at the party: "I thank you for taking in my sons and teaching them how to live in Eretz-Israel. But we are a kind of kibbutz ourselves, and after my sons finish their army service, we will all go together." — *"Her children rise up, and call her blessed."*

Where should they go? In those days, people had begun to speak of Lachish, awakening from a sleep of thousands of years. The brothers applied to the Jewish Agency with a special request: to assign them six farms on the edge of one of the new villages in the Lachish region, for they wished to establish a "village within a village."

There were many doubts as to their project: one of the brothers was still in Morocco, and the five brothers in the country were all still unmarried — and therefore 'unstable' human material, in the light of previous experience. To their good fortune, the region head was a bold man, capable of diverging from routine procedure. He examined them closely, asking them many questions, and all the sons gave the same answer: "We have a mother, and she makes the decisions. We all obey her." She was victorious. *"She considereth a field, and buyeth it."*

The Ben-Tolila family settled in Shakhar. Yaakov, the eldest, also immigrated to Israel with his wife and children, and he found everything "ready and waiting". With the money Yaakov brought with him from the sale of his property in Morocco they bought two tractors and other implements necessary for the farm. All the family finances were in a common fund. Each of the brothers was responsible for a separate branch — vegetables, green fodder, chickens, sheep, machinery. In the evenings, around the large table, the "parliament" of Ben-Tolila, as their mother called them, would assemble for a meeting. She herself would take an active part in political discussions, as she had during her husband's lifetime: her husband was an educated man, active in public affairs. Today the "wise men" of Shakhar gather in their house and hold lively discussions on current events. The mother's busy hands embroider or knit. The little granddaughter, Rivka, who greatly resembles her grandmother, clings to her lovingly.

Not long ago, the distinguished widow held a wedding celebration for her third son. The son was worried about his mother working too hard and suggested that they hold the wedding in one of the cafés in the city, according to the modern custom.

His mother answered shortly: "If you like, but without me!"

"Forget what I said," replied the son.

For two months the mother toiled incessantly: she sewed magnificent dresses for the bride, for her two daughters-in-law, and for the "little bride" — her granddaughter, Rivka — who was dressed, according to the custom of the Sephardim, in the clothes of a bride, and who held the bride's train as she was led beneath the bridal canopy. And, of course, she sewed herself a suitable dress for the occasion.

The evening before the wedding ceremony, the traditional ceremony of the bride's reception was held in the house. After the bride had gone to the ritual bath she was dressed in a special dress, one that has passed from generation to generation in the Ben-Tolila family. The heavy dress is made of velvet, and is completely covered with embroidery of gold thread. The bride was crowned with a high coronet, studded with precious stones and pearls, beneath which flared a cloth-of-gold veil.

In honour of the bride, a litter was prepared. It was covered with glistening white silk, its poles ornamented, and on its canopy was the inscription: "*The voice of the bridegroom and the voice of the bride.*" Beneath the canopy, a "throne" for the bride, and two other seats, one on either side.

The bride was led through the multitude with lighted candles. The bride, incidentally, was the ninth of a dozen sisters in a family of thirteen children. The elders of the community accompanied her with the song "*A graceful doe*" and with verses from the Song of Songs. They then seated her beneath the canopy, and the two mothers, the mother of the bridegroom and the mother of the bride, were seated on either side. The guests sat around her, partaking of refreshments and feasting their eyes with the sight of the fabulous dress that recalled the magnificent weddings of the Jews of Morocco — the 'dress of happiness' of the mothers of the community, a dress in which no woman had ever aged, or died.

After the wedding, on the eve of the Sabbath, the married sons took post in the usual Sabbath reception in their mother's house. Another family has been added to Israel, despite all that the evil nations have done to us. The blessing and prayers were repeated, and the sons sang to their mother and to their wives, in a chorus: "*Who can find a virtuous woman? For her price is far above rubies.*"

XVII

JEWS OF ABRAHAM THE PATRIARCH

THE VILLAGE of Otsem, on the ridge of the hill south of the Iraq-Suidan highway, opened a new page in the history of the settlement of the country on May 22 ,1955: the settlement of the Lachish region. To Otsem came immigrants from Bugmez, in the Atlas mountains.

These Jews did not come to Israel owing to Moslem persecution, or because of economic advantages. They had been dwelling in the mountainous area of north Africa even before Islam penetrated to Morocco. The inhabitants of the area are Berbers, engaged in agriculture. The Jews engaged in crafts and trades. The two communities had mutual ties by reason of their respective occupations, and relations between them were always good; but by chance the report of the renewed existence of the State of Israel reached the Jews of Bugmez. A young rabbi, who had come from the city of Marrakech to guide the spiritual lives of the Jews who lived in the mountains, brought the isolated community news of the revival of an independent Israel.

Yehuda Grinker, from Nahalal, discovered the Jews of Bugmez with something of the same feeling Columbus must have had when he discovered America. Two of them appeared in the offices of the Jewish Agency in Casablanca. They made an unforgettable impression on everyone present: tall, powerful, wrapped in white robes with peaked hoods, noble faces wreathed with beards — "Jews of Abraham the Patriarch".

Bracha Habas describes the meeting between the Israeli officials and these Jews from beyond the Mountains of Darkness:

"... After this meeting, the Agency workers made their way into the mountains. The entire trip was a marvel. The mountains were the height of the Alps, separated by gorges and valleys, and in the heart of the mountains a Jewish village was revealed. When it became known in the village that the guests had come from Eretz-Israel, there was great rejoicing. They hastened to bring a man who knew Hebrew. He invited the guests to his house. The house was impeccably clean. The guests were welcomed and feasted. When they left the house, they found all the inhabitants of the village waiting for them, bundles on their shoulders and staffs in their hands. Astonished, the young men from Eretz-Israel asked the meaning of the sight, and they were informed that these Jews, thirsty for redemption, had taken their words literally. They were certain that the messengers from the Holy Land had come to take them with them to Jerusalem, of course. So here they were, ready and waiting..."

One of the Israelis who had been present at that meeting told me that the Jews of the village had encircled them, marching around them seven times, singing psalms and crying out: "The Messiah is coming!"

The report that the Jews were leaving Bugmez horrified their Berber neighbours, who also threatened the Israelis and declared that they would under no circumstances permit the Jews to leave the homes where they had dwelled for hundreds of years in amity with the natives of the country. But great is the power of the dream of a homeland. In small groups, under military escort, the Jews of Bugmez stole away, and in this fashion they all immigrated to the Promised Land.

Adjustment to their new homeland was hard for them. They encountered many disappointments. The rabbi of the community once told us: "The trouble with the State is that it has no believers, and the laws of the Torah are not observed in the land of the patriarchs..."

The community passed through a difficult spiritual crisis. For generation upon generation, these families had been educated in respect for parents and elders, patriarchal hospitality strict observance of the Sabbath; and here in Israel, their entire world was being destroyed. They would shudder when they would see one of their sons, home on a short leave from the army, riding a bicycle on the Sabbath; or when a young bride would declare, after the wedding, that she didn't want to live with her mother-in-law. Formerly, the young husband would have proven the strength of his arm to her, and with that, would have ended all her complaints. Incidentally, the Jews of Bugmez are the quietest and most law-abiding of all the various communities of Eastern Jews, and the disputes which occur among them never end in physical violence. This, however, does not apply to the wife of their bosom, whom they are in the habit of 'convincing' with hearty blows, while she dares not even question the "right" of her husband to do so. In recent years there have been instances where the wife complained to the woman instructor. Nevertheless, in the opinion of the rabbi of Otsem, the women have become "shameless".

The settlers of Otsem are more religious than those of the other villages. Their children did not join the public school at Nehora, but chose to travel to the religious school in distant Telamim. Yet many superstitions have also clung to them, and the people still keep their unique customs. Before a circumcision, mysterious symbols are drawn in soot on the face of the newborn infant. The rabbi is called to a sickbed to read psalms, and also to make magic incantations. At a wedding, at the end of the feast, the father of the bride takes her on his shoulder (if necessary, he is given help) and ceremoniously carries her to the house of the bridegroom and seats her on the covered bed, beside her husband.

The people of Otsem are wonderfully hospitable, as was Abraham the Patriarch in his day, and in their eyes there is no greater insult than for a guest to refuse to taste the delicacies offered him by his host. The sociologist Miriam Golani, who visited every house in the village while doing research on this community, writes:

"... After his wife had told me of her troubles, the husband also told me his. After several hours, the husband wished to emphasize his feelings of friendliness towards me. He took out a small package and asked me to refresh myself with a unique beverage, one which could not be had in this country at any price, and which he had just recently received from a new immigrant from Morocco. I was served with black coffee that almost knocked me unconscious: it was coffee mixed with pepper..."

If their neighbours from Bugmez could see the people of Otsem now, they would no longer recognize them as natives of the mountains. The same women who were afraid to light a simple kerosene burner and continued to bake their *pita* in a '*prina*' — a low oven made of packed clay — have today already exchanged their kerosene camp stoves for gas stoves in almost every house, as have the women of the other villages in the Lachish region. In Lachish they say that the gas stove has done what no woman instructor ever succeeded in doing: it has raised up the daughter of the East from the floor. Today the young woman works in her kitchen standing up in front of the modern kitchen sink, and she eats together with her family, sitting down at the table. Except for the very old, the people of the village have almost been weaned from their habit of sitting on mats on the floor.

The houses are very clean, and all furnished in exactly the same style: no self-respecting man would let himself be outdone by his neighbour. Shiny wardrobes, a table and four upholstered chairs, a double sofa — although the husband and wife continue to sleep in the narrow beds supplied to them by the Agency on their arrival in the country. In a corner stands a special bed — an 'unclean' bed — in which the wife sleeps apart during certain periods. There is also a modern crib for the baby, although at night he still sleeps with his mother.

The people of Otsem served as the first guinea-pigs for the

"ship-to-settlement" immigration, and without doubt the team of village workers played a great part in the absorption of this very special human material. Not without reason did these immigrants feel such a great affection for their first instructor. In Lachish in those days it was said in jest: "The Bugmezis are afraid of two things: of signing their names to a piece of paper, and of their instructor leaving..."

The religious parties attempted to convince the people of Otsem to change from *Tnuat Hamoshavim* to "Hapoel Hamizrachi", and they even succeeded in dividing the village: fourteen families moved to another village. But Otsem overcame even this severe crisis, and today it is regarded as one of the well-established villages in Lachish. The birth rate and the cotton yields are among the highest in this area. During the week of Pesach in 1957 four sons were born in Otsem, Four households celebrated the *brit-milah* of their sons, and the hearts of the Bugmezis swelled with pride.

There is no halting the process of assimilation among the new immigrants. It is unavoidable, and is most apparent in its external forms: changes in the mode of dress and in standard of living. Only a few old men still study in the books of "Zohar", printed in Vilna that had reached the Atlas mountains in some mysterious way. But when the old way of life and its deeply-rooted traditions clash with the new world — the clashes are frequently accompanied by excitement and disturbances.

Two years ago the entire country was in an uproar over the affair of the '*yibum*' in Otsem. The nephew of the rabbi of the community, an young man of eighteen, died of heart disease. He had been married for two years to a girl of his own age. (In Bugmez, marriage took place at a very early age: in 1955, there were two married pupils in the third grade of the school at Otsem, who wore head-coverings.)

The young man had suffered from his mortal disease since the day he had been born, and the poor girl was condemned to a life with a kind of 'living dead man'. However, after his death, her situation was worsened: she had no children, and therefore she was obligated to marry legally, but for three days only, the elder brother of her husband, so that she might give birth to a son to be named after her dead husband. This brother was the father of three children.

'*Yibum*' is one of the accepted customs in their native land. But the young woman instructor working in Otsem at the time moved mountains in order to release the widow from this cruel and primitive custom. It was necessary that the widow receive (a release) *'khalitza'* from the dead husband's brother. However, the rabbi did not agree to this, and the entire village was on his side. In the opinion of the elders, *'yibum'* was a commandment to be honoured, as it is set down in the Torah. (Deuteronomy, 25, 5). From the *'yibum'* the brother's seed is raised up, and the family is enlarged. The soul of the dead man will enter the Garden of Eden if his son says *'kaddish'* for him.

The newspapers pounced on the story, published articles and printed the photographs of everyone concerned, and especially of the younger brother of the dead husband — a boy of nine, who faced the camera with his finger in his mouth like someone who is not at all in a hurry. According to the law, this boy was the only member of the family who could save the widow of his brother from marrying a man who was already married: when he reached maturity he could marry his brother's wife, or give her a *'khalitza'*.

I took part in one of the discussions about the *'yibum'* with the rabbi himself. He sat facing us — a scholar of the Torah, distinguished looking and extremely courteous. It was apparent that he was suffering from this vulgar interference in affairs which were incomprehensible to strangers.

We put pressure on him: Why, all the same, is the brother so set in his refusal to give *'khalitza'* to the widow? Is it not permissible, according to the laws of our sacred Torah?

The rabbi replied in the voice of a suffering man:

"How can he act in such a fashion?! Why, the woman would have to *spit* in his face, and what would people call him? They would call him: *he who hath his shoe loosed!*"★

★ The ceremony of *khalitza* requires that the woman concerned remove the shoe of the man who is refusing to carry out his family responsibilities by not marrying her — the woman's loosening his shoe is a symbol of this refusal of responsibility, a formal and public condemnation of the man, regarded as a deepdisgrace to him. The ceremony also requires the woman to spit in his face — a universal mark of contempt and for an Eastern Jew intensified by the fact that it is a *woman* who spits in his face, with the full approval of the community.

I recalled Bialik's poem, *"To the Daughters of Shfeya."* In this poem the poet expresses his fatherly feelings of pity for the orphans of Shfeya, and he warns every decent young man not to harm the defenceless girls of Shfeya:

But woe unto you, son of Belial,
If you shame the daughters of your people in Shfeya;
No more will you be a husband among your people,
"Go!" They will say to you — "Go, he who hath his shoe loosed!
Take your belongings and go!"

Bialik, who was well-versed in the whole of Hebrew literature, apparently found no more insulting expression for the concept of "defiler of Israel" than the expression "he who hath his shoe loosed".

The culture and the rigid traditions of the Jews of Bugmez kept them from assimilating into the tribes of the Berbers during the hundreds of years they lived in the Atlas mountains. Within that tradition, they raised sons who are devoted to their parents and loyal to their people. The Bugamazim brought their own customs and a well-defined way of life with them to Israel, together with fearful ignorance of the ways of the the modern world.

We will never see these Jews among the immigrants who leave Israel. How can we find the right way to add to their knowledge, and at the same time preserve their full spiritual stature?

XVIII

BIRTH PANGS OF THE VILLAGE CENTRE

We moved to our permanent house in the new village centre of Nehora with regret. During the years that had passed since the War of Independence, we had not experienced as satisfying a year as the one we had spent in Noga, a year of full lives and spiritual peace.

On the first Sabbath after we moved to Nehora, Noga surprised us: from morning till evening the procession did not cease; all the men of the village, accompanied by their wives, felt themselves obliged to congratulate us on our new house. Not a man came with empty hands: they brought us many presents, and, after the Eastern custom, filled our new home with gifts of sugar and honey, which sweetened our lives for some time afterwards.

One of the gifts made a strong impression on us: a large picture, in eye-opening colours, which represented a woman, pink and sturdy, wrapped in the filmiest of material, reclining in a boat, with a band of cherubs surrounding her. Was *anything* lacking in that picture? It had water, skies, clouds and a sunset, trees and every imaginable flower! It was clear that this present was the gift of a full heart.

Even the man who had not yet forgotten the "trickery" — the clothes I had once sewn for his children — came with his wife, and brought us six decorated glass plates. I guard them faithfully, for who can weigh the spiritual effort it must have cost him to make the decision to waste his money on such luxurious items.

But the nicest present we received came from Matanah — the close friend I had made in Noga, of whom I am very fond. The lovely Matanah, mother of ten, noble and shy, sang in our house! In her thin, delicate voice, she sang a Kurdish song in our honour, with a dovelike moan.

Two years later, Ethel Sussman, daughter of our friends and a well-known singer, paid us a visit. She was visiting the country in order to appear with the Israel Philharmonic orchestra at the opening celebration of the tenth year of Israel's independence. This artist, who had grown up in the country and now lived in France, was deeply affected by Lachish. When she visited us, she was greatly stirred, and she expressed her feelings in her own way: she sang to us.

The little house filled with notes that would have taken the breath of tens of thousands of people in the concert halls of the world's capitals. It did not surprise me: I felt that the great singer was answering the echo of Matanah's voice, which still resounded.

The situation facing us was not bright: Mordecai was given the task of establishing services for the fourteen villages in the area, supplying the educational, cultural, and medical needs, in addition to coordinating the civic administration of this entire population. I was assigned the task of administering the school that served seven of the region's villages.

I had many qualms about accepting this responsibility. Before school opened, I paid a visit to the President's home and told Yitzchak Ben-Zvi and his wife about my doubts as to my ability to head an educational institution for hundreds of children from various countries, when I had at my disposal only a staff of inexperienced teachers.

The President of the State of Israel said:

"*Go in this thy might!*"

In Karel Capek's play, "The Mother", the mother tells her dead husband, in an imaginary conversation: "Do you know what it is to raise five children? It means shoes, books, medicines, grades, and again shoes..."

I had similar problems. More than anything else, I was worried about whether they would finish painting the woodwork and putting glass in the windows before the beginning of the school year. It was exasperating that the blackboards had not been hung at the right height, among other things. A friend from Tel Aviv, Bracha Livneh, volunteered to make two hundred pairs of warm slippers. This meant a greal deal, for cleanliness is the basis of every civilized culture, and one of the characteristics that differentiates man from beast. But how could we maintain cleanliness in the large classrooms on a rainy day, when there was mud outside, and the children had only one pair of shoes?

Nehora filled with residents slowly and with difficulty, as had Noga in its day. Two families, ours and that of Menachem, Mordecai's secretary, the doctor and the nurse and another five families of the workers at the tractor station comprised the entire population of the village centre until school opened. I was already acquainted with the teachers who were to work in the school. Most of them were soldiers who had spent the previous year working in the villages of the area. During the second year of their army service, each came with her pupils to the new school in Nehora. Only one new teacher was sent to us by the Department of Education.

The anthem of Lachish begins with the words: "For thousands of years, there was only desert here" — and so, already a real school was being opened — sturdy buildings, suitable equipment, and a teacher for every grade! Was it any wonder that we had broken Rose's car trying to get trees planted in the schoolyard as soon as possible? I did everything I could to wipe out all traces of 'temporary arrangements'. My pupils from Noga, the nearest village to the centre, took an active part in these preparations.

On my return from Jerusalem, after attending a study course

for a month, I called my class together, and together we decided on a plan of action. We planned every detail. Even before there was a school janitor — in Noga, we had refused the hired worker usually supplied by the Department of Education, and had done the work ourselves — the children carted away the building refuse, planted the first trees and fenced them in, and made paths through the schoolyard, using the sand and gravel left over from the construction work. The library occupied only a small room, but already it contained over a thousand books, selected and catalogued, and it was ready to serve the teachers and pupils. The teachers' room was transformed into a charming corner, and around it the first flowers were planted. The children watered them from watering-cans, for the pipe line had not yet been laid to the school.

In the month of August I sent a personal letter to each of the teachers. I asked them to come two days before school opened. During my years of work in immigrant settlements, I had grown used to seeing the identical scene repeated on the first day of school: teachers and pupils running to and fro, searching for the keys or for some other necessary equipment. I wanted to prevent this confusion, and to make the first day in the first regional school in the first village centre "after two thousand years", etc. — something worthy of the name. The young women teachers responded, and they all arrived on Thursday evening. The school was to open on Sunday. We accommodated the young women, all of whom were unmarried, in the two houses set aside for them. On Friday morning we started work — I was familiar with this through my work in the school of the *ma'abara* in Qastina. To each teacher I distributed textbooks, pencils, notebooks, and other equipment — each item was like a small bolt, without which the entire machinery might easily become paralysed. The teachers also asked for papers and paints to decorate the classrooms.

I myself went back home to prepare a meal for the Sabbath Eve for all the large family that had assembled. The young teachers remained in the schoolhouse and worked there the whole day. When I went back to the school in the late afternoon, I stood openmouthed with astonishment. Across the entire width of the central building stretched a huge inscription: "The Regional School in Lachish Welcomes Its Pupils On The First Day of School". Each door had a neat sign bearing the number of the grade, and every classroom was beautifully arranged. A cheerful new curtain hung in the library, painted with comic figures. On the rough material she had been given, one of the teachers had painted a menagerie of "readers": an elephant holding a book upside down, a hen laying an egg on a book, and a goat eating one.

I thought to myself: "*For thy law is my delight*". The young teachers were entertaining themselves, and they rivalled one another in their good taste and clever handiwork, through love for the children. You have defeated me, my daughters!

That Sabbath Eve was unique. The young teachers refreshed my heart with their song and their cheerfulness. Together, they seemed like living flowers.

On the Sabbath the girls rested and went for a hike. In the evening they told me that the new teacher — a young man — had also arrived, and accommodation had to be found for him. I went to meet him, and found him surrounded by the young women.

I made a great mistake: I told him proudly of the young women's practical talents.

The young man instantly replied: "Why should they have done it? Where does a teacher start working two days before the first of September? It's not legal! I've come before the appointed time, too, I have no obligation whatsoever to report here before eight o'clock tomorrow morning."

The young man was tall and handsome, and in any case looked down on me.

The girls hesitated only a moment, but the common age and interests were decisive — and I knew that I must do battle with that intangible factor that was leaking in through the cracks and gaps, the thing called "the spirit of the times." The young man lived by rules that were easy to obey. I felt as though some destructive weed had gotten into the field where we worked, and that it might take root and spread over the fertile plot.

XIX

I'M A "WELFARE CASE" TOO...

Ever since I encountered the Indians, who paid a visit to Nehora, members of the "Buddhan" movement who beg donations of land for poor, landless farmers, I have begun to feel as though we, the descendants of the prophets, have sunk into an exaggerated materialism, and the code of our prophets, together with our spiritual heritage from A.D. Gordon and Brenner, seems to have abandoned us and moved to distant India...

I asked one of the guests, whose sole garment was a sheet and whose diet consisted of tiny portions of the simplest foods, about his activities.

"Why do you wander from one place to another, and make such long journeys, and go such enormous distances on foot instead of passing a law in your parliament transferring the superfluous lands of the rich into the hands of the poor?"

The face of the dark-skinned man seemed to glow with an inner light. He shook his head and replied in calm content:

"What Man would consent to profit by something that has been taken from his brother by force?"

We went forth to welcome the mass immigration equipped mainly with good will, but at the same time our hands held almost nothing that was actual. We quickly understood that the devoted care given to people who had never in their lives experienced such a thing produced bad results more than once: the people under our care grew spoiled and began to behave with undue self-importance. We duplicated the errors of farmers who over-irrigate their groves — and thereby ruin them; with too much cultivation, the tree does not put down deep roots and will not be able to absorb its nourishment independently in the future, nor will it withstand natural pests and diseases. No happiness in the world equals that of the human selfconfidence that springs from lack of dependence on the aid of one's fellow man.

I have already told of the two blind old women who came with the other members of their family to the *ma'abara* of Qastina at the beginning of the mass immigration, and who never dreamed of regarding themselves as a public responsibility. I feared that the burden was too great for the poor family that dwelled in a tent, and I suggested transferring the old women to a public institution. The family pitied them and did not agree, for the two blind old women would have been lonely and solitary in a strange place. I am certain that these two old women did, indeed, live out their days in the bosom of their family.

But — 'The air of Eretz-Israel makes one wise . . .' The new immigrants rapidly learned to demand and get "what's coming to them", and as a result we have seen aged men and women — even in traditional communities, whose children have been raised to honour and care for their parents — deserted and abandoned to the charity of their fellow creatures.

As a general rule the welfare office is incapable of giving a person from the Eastern communities the same degree of security and mutual aid that was given to him by his united family circle in his country of origin.

A family of Persian immigrants settled in Noga, a mother and seven children. The youngest daughter, today a pupil in tenth grade, was three months old when the father of the family died. This mother resembles Rivka Ben-Tolila, who is so respected throughout Lachish, in her tall stature and her capability in raising a productive, united family by herself. I visited this woman in her home many times. She was hardworking, and aroused admiration with her well-balanced personality, her self-respect, and her strong determination not to be dependent upon the charity of others. Her husband was a goldsmith — one of the commonest trades among the Jews of Iranian Kurdistan. He used to journey into the mountains for months on end to repair the ornaments of the wives of the Arabs who lived in the isolated villages. He would come home for the holidays, bringing a little money and a little food he had received in payment for his work. From one of these journeys he did not return. Apparently the Arabs coveted the precious metal he carried with him. He vanished without a trace. After all, he was only a Jew, and who would avenge his blood? . . .

"And how did you raise seven children by yourself?"

"I didn't raise them by myself. 'A one-armed man does not clap hands'.* My father was still alive. Later on, we lived together with the family of my uncle. At first my uncle would not permit me to come here. He said, "I am an old man, it is not in my power to go with you. And who will watch over you, who will teach your sons to respect you?" I told him: 'My sons already have enough sense. They want to go to Eretz-Israel, and I won't let them be orphans there' . . ."

And thus the widow Khotmi reached the Agrobank *ma'-abara* and from there she came to the immigrant village in Lachish. Today her sons cultivate four farms in Noga, and her married daughter is the mistress of a farm in one of the moshavim in the Negev.

No one would recognize a poor widow in this erect woman who dresses carefully and acts with full consciousness of her own importance. Moreover, there is not a sign of 'orphanhood' in her youngest daughter, a smart, lively girl of sixteen, a pupil in high school and one of the best-dressed girls in the village.

When I was working in the settlements of the Negev, all the women of the village would gather around me and quarrel among themselves over who was to have the privilege of having me as a guest in her home. I rejoiced at their warm

---
* A Kurdish proverb

welcome until it became clear that their welcome was intended mainly for the handbag I carried with me. In this handbag I kept the sweets and toys with which I was supplied by the President's wife. The women of the village had an exaggerated idea of my resources and were certain that I had the power of lavishing on them far greater gifts. I once visited the house of a Yemenite in an immigrant village. His thin, faded wife immediately sounded the familiar chorus after every sentence: "It's a pity on us!...."

"— This is a life? No paved road, dust in the house, no electricity... in Haifa, in Tel Aviv, things are good! Really, lady, it's a pity on us!...."

Her husband raised his head from the prayer book and winked at me.

"Don't listen to her, she wants a wardrobe," he said, and began to scold his wife. "What do you want from her? She doesn't have anything!"

"She has!" she insisted. "She has, she'll give it to us!"

With the settlement of the new region, many welfare cases also arrived, requiring aid from the welfare office. It was hard to decide in which cases the aid helped and in which cases it only did harm. Cases were discovered that had no parallel in any Jewish community from any Eastern country. In one case, after a family quarrel, the wife left her husband with three children, and once even with four small children. The social worker started a search for one of these "runaways" and found her staying with her sister, who lived with her large own family in a dark hovel in the ruins of an abandoned Arab village. The woman would travel long distances, to the city, to scrub floors in order to earn her living.

The social worker asked her, "Who have you left to care for your children?"

She replied at once, "The children aren't mine, they're Ben-Gurion's."

And thus Ben-Gurion became, without knowing it, the "father" of abandoned children...

Families with numerous children live in conditions of demoralizing overcrowding in housing we built for them according to our idea of the size of a family. An enormous gap exists between the citizens of our country in level of education and standard of living, and this inequality threatens our very existence.

We ourselves and the new citizens of the country have gotten used to "handouts". This is, indeed, an evil habit in principle, but it is the lesser evil. Could we dress all the children shivering with cold (and there are very many) without using the supply of clothing from America? How could we cope with the tragedies, illnesses and other catastrophes without the welfare office?

Unfortunately, we have no means of preventing the spiritual damage done to a man who receives aid and himself gives nothing in return. And we are still in ignorance as to the exact point where we should cut off all aid and abandon the man to his fate — so that he learn to help himself.

The aged Shimka is one of our old friends in Noga. The man was a caretaker in the synagogue of his native city, Kweisanzak, in Iraq. His entire appearance speaks of self-respect and consideration for his fellow man, as a man who has been accustomed to caring for the needs of scholars all his life. He did not change his mode of dress. He continues to wear a *kombaz* and to wrap his head in a *tarbush*. In Noga he has dozens of grandchildren and great-grandchildren — but he will not consent to go and live with one of his sons. They all moved to permanent houses, but he and his second wife continue to live in a hut. The Area Council has found 'relief work' for him, and he earns his meagre living honestly, as a faithful worker. It made us uncomfortable for an old man to have to work with a heavy *turiya* and earn his living by the sweat of his brow. At last he began to receive the national insurance pension given to people of his age, and in the evening of his life he became a man whose modest support was assured him: fifty pounds a month.

We wondered what the aged Shimka would do now. He travelled to Jerusalem to visit his relatives, and to bow down before the grave of King David on Mount Zion. He brought back gifts to his smaller grandchildren and his great-grandchildren, as well as to our daughter and to the son of the secretary, Menachem. On Saturday night, the old man, accompanied by his wife, appeared at the weekly movie: apparently he had at last decided to enjoy the pleasures of this world. Shimka sat there, erect and serious as usual, and looked at the screen for two hours without batting an eye. Who knows what impression the passions of Hollywood and its stars made on him, as they passed before his eyes?

The next morning Shimka reported to the Council office and asked for work; his request was granted.

Once I summoned one of the parents to school to inform him of his son's bad behaviour. The boy had been teasing a cripple who was well-known to the children of the village. The man would often appear in front of the social welfare office, which was next to the schoolyard, and sit down on the steps like a man whose time is his own.

I wanted to make the father understand what a great wrong his son was doing the cripple.

"He's an unfortunate man," I said. "A 'welfare case'!"

The father smiled with modest pride, and commented, so that his honour would suffer no damage:

"I'm a welfare case too!"

At the same time the aged Shimka was swinging his heavy *turiya* and hoeing around the trees that stood in front of the teachers' room, where this odd conversation was taking place...

I recall an incident that occurred to me in the days when I was visiting the settlements on the 'Famine Road'. Once I was travelling from village to village in the wagon of a Yemenite settler who had a beard and side-curls. On the way, the Yemenite began to tell me his troubles: his wife was no good, all she had given him was five daughters. The eldest daughter, who was fourteen, wasn't going to school any longer. She was working in the Jewish Agency nursery in Gilat and supporting the whole family. The farm wasn't bringing in anything, because there wasn't anyone to work on it. I comforted him as best I could: his daughters would grow up, with God's help, and marry husbands, and then the farm would also be redeemed.

The Yemenite smiled at my enthusiastic words and said dubiously:

"Yes, then we'll rest, we'll rest..."

A large herd of sheep and goats blocked the road in front of us. A small, odd figure strode behind them, waving a knotted staff. When we drew near the herd, I could not tell whether it was a man or a woman..

The Yemenite who wanted to marry off his daughters and rest from the heavy toil of life told me with great interest that this was the shepherdess of the neighbouring village of Bitkha, and she was also a Yemenite.

"She's already very, very old — maybe seventy, maybe eighty! And ever since she was a child, still in Yemen, she's been a shepherdess..."

In rain and cold, in the sandstorms of the Negev, from dawn till dark, on Sabbath and holiday, the aged shepherdess strode behind her flocks for decades. She finds her way in the plains, and knows no fear. Many times she has encountered infiltrators, and has gotten safely away without having even one sheep taken from her. She is paid two grush (or agorot) per head, and if any of the flock is lost, the loss is taken out of her wages, as the Torah has it: *"That which was torn of beasts I brought not unto thee; I bare the loss of it; of my hand didst thou require it..."*

Only on the Day of Atonement did the shepherdess dress in festive clothes, kept in her house since the days of her wedding, and go to the synagogue. With her salary she supports her only son, who has not been successful with his farm. Now, when we met her, she had a bundle of branches tied to her back, which she had gathered for fuel. When she crossed the road again and passed before us, waving her staff in the air, the ancient woman seemed to me like a living reprimand to many of those crowding around the doors of the welfare offices.

XX

DURING THE SINAI CAMPAIGN

The school year had just begun, when suddenly — with no advance warning, and without our having heard even one shot fired — the Sinai Campaign exploded, and we found ourselves in a state of emergency. All men in Nehora were mobilized, and their wives were left alone with the children. We now learned that every member of Nehora was a 'goodly young man': one was a seaman, one a pilot, one a tank driver — we found ourselves suitably represented in all branches of the armed forces.

The regional school in Nehora was disbanded. Who would think of taking children any distance away from their parents at a time like this? The young women soldier-teachers were despatched in pairs to each village. I, too, returned to Noga with one other teacher, to the same pupils I had taught the previous year.

In the morning we sat in the same hut where I had first assembled the children over a year ago, when some of them had wanted to sit on the tables and others had preferred to knock on the wooden walls outside. Everything was as impermanent now as it was then, but a change had taken place in the children sitting at the tables, and we had become attached to one another.

Lachish now proved its importance from a security standpoint. The Lachish settlement project had been undertaken primarily because of the demands of national defence; the rapid development of the region had been implemented and guided not by economic considerations, but by the security requirements of the country. The army gave priority not to the section of Lachish adjoining the border, near the mountains of Hebron, but to the settlement of the low-lying area — the wide plain stretching between Negba and Bror Khayil.

Before the Lachish region was settled in the summer of 1955 this area was almost uninhabited. In the event of the "second round" that was a constant potential danger, the Egyptian army would have been able to move through the Lachish region, from Gaza to Hebron, with almost no resistance. We now realized the enormous value of the rapid settlement project in the Lachish region. During a single year, this settlement placed heavy obstacles in the path of any potential invader: more than twenty agricultural settlements and a well-populated city.

During the Sinai Campaign only three men were left in Nehora, all of whom had been rejected on medical grounds by the army: Mordecai who was overage at 64, and two young men who were physically handicapped; one of them was our driver, and the second was the janitor of the school. These three men were the only armed guards in the village centre of Nehora, where a dozen women and children had been left. In those days the area was crawling with *fedayin,* Egyptian-trained infiltrators despatched from their base in Gaza on missions of sabotage and murder.

Mordecai was responsible for the supply of food and other necessities to all the villages in the area. All the settlers were ordered to dig trenches beside their houses. Emergency committees were formed. Instructions had to be given to the settlers of each separate village, as all the permanent instructors had been called up and were at the front. Arrangements had to be made for repair of the public air raid shelters, taping the windows, maintaining a complete blackout, and sounding an alarm in case of danger.

During the eighteen months we had lived in Lachish we had grown used to the constant tension: shots were frequently heard in the area at night. We were used to seeing soldiers and tanks on the roads. But only now did we realize the importance of a radio set in keeping us in contact with the outside world. My transistor was out of order. Four years ago, there were no transistors in the country.

Noga and Nehora adjoined one another, with only the highway between them. Despite the location of the two villages, I did not see Mordecai for several days in a row, nor did I get a note from him every day.

Every night there was some new problem in Noga. There was also a tragedy. Late one afternoon Mordecai sent the janitor of the school from Nehora to Noga to get an extra rifle. It was just at sundown. The messenger took a shortcut and made his way through one of the farmyards.

The people of Noga were disturbed by the many irresponsibly-spread rumours and horror stories. The owner of the farm, alarmed when a man suddenly appeared in his yard, shot him twice at close range and wounded him gravely.

At the sound of the shots the alarm was sounded, the people began running to the shelters, and the children increased the confusion by shouting about an Egyptian column approaching with tanks, which they thought they had seen on the horizon.

Suddenly a woman came running up and cried, "Come quick! It's a Jew, on the Torah! He's lying by our clover field. They've killed him..."

I ran to the spot and found the janitor, Yechiel, lying in a pool of blood. He was wounded in the chest and in the shoulder. It was a difficult feat to get him to the Kaplan Hospital that same night; and it was no easier to inform his wife, who was waiting for him with their three children and worrying over his safety, for he had supposedly left the house for only a short time — and to convince her that he was alive and no longer in danger.

Almost none of the men of Noga were called up. The army certainly had its own reasons: the security of the village, concern for the crops. As to the education of the new immigrants in fulfilling their civic duties, a policy was adopted that had its source in the Bible: "*What man is there that hath built a new house, and hath not dedicated it ... And what man is there that hath planted a vineyard and hath not yet eaten of it ... Let him go and return to his house ...*" In most cases, the establishment of house and vineyard has gone on for five years.

The few settlers who were called up and went to the army did so in low spirits, and the village looked upon them with pity, as though they had been condemned to die. In the days of the fighting, I heard that one of the young men in the village, married and the father of two children, had received an order to report for duty. I went to his house and found him parting from his family. The yard was filled with friends, and dozens of children crowded in from the street. It was a heart-rending scene: all of them were weeping and wailing at the top of their lungs. The soldier's wife prostrated herself in the dust and embraced his feet. His mother rent her clothes and tore her hair. Indeed, it was enough to melt the heart of the boldest warrior.

Fortunately, "Solel Boneh", the construction company, completed the construction of our houses before the Sinai Campaign began, and all the families were accommodated in concrete houses equipped with iron shutters that had security bolts. These shutters, which increased the expense of construction enormously, were approved by the Settlement Authority only for the Lachish region, where every house was a kind of miniature fortress.

Again I was living in Noga, this time alone. I taped the windows in my room, and at night I listened to the hum of the airplanes which were constantly flying over us. It was hard to remember that only eight years had passed since the days when every plane that appeared in the sky was an enemy plane, and shells from the Egyptian artillery on the roof of the Iraq-

Suidan police station landed in Kfar Warburg and threatened to flatten every settlement in the area, while now I was living in a village of new immigrants east of the terrible police station, and the airplanes above us were ours — our shield and sword against any enemy.

Suddenly I heard the alarm outside. The village commander of Noga sent messengers with urgent orders to get all the settlers into the two public shelters in the centre of the village. On the field telephone we received a report that there was a unit of *Fedayin* in the area who had just attacked a house in the neighbouring village and badly wounded one of the settlers. A cleaning-up operation was being carried out by the army, and it would be safer for the settlers to keep inside the shelters.

It is almost impossible to describe the scene of the women with all their children, awakened by an alarm at midnight to take refuge underground. There were only four women to take charge of the entire group. We distributed the duties among ourselves: the nurse and the young woman teacher went to one shelter; I and another young woman soldier, a daughter of Kibbutz Tel Yosef who was working as an instructor in pre-military training for the young people, went to the other shelter.

The women and children pushed one another on the steps leading down into the shelter. No one would relinquish his seating space on the floor, not even for an old man. Finally people began to faint, owing to the foul air and poor ventilation. We discovered that the shelter had not been equipped with a pipeline. The young woman soldier and I went out to bring water. The settlers were afraid to take even one step outside the shelter to help us find a nearby faucet in the dark. The girl and I went back and forth dozens of times to bring drinking water for the thirsty.

Behind the shelter there were shadows — figures with rifles — that frightened us, until we found that they were the guards who were supposed to have been on emergency watch on all sides of the village. They announced that as all the women and children were in the shelters, they would not move from the spot at any price.

Just before dawn the signal was given to return to the houses, and we were informed that not a single thing had happened in the Lachish region that night, and all the panic had been over a false alarm. The children came to school later than usual, their faces grey from their sleepless night. Their first question was:

"Teacher, don't you know what they're saying on the radio?"

Two weeks later I paid a visit to the house of the soldier who had been sent off with laments and mourning when he went to the front. He was home on leave from the Sinai desert, and he told us about the battles and the victories. The house was again filled with relatives, neighbours and friends. They all crowded around the hero, gazing at him with loving eyes and drinking in his words. They did not cease to praise the God of Israel and to offer thanks to Him for the miracles He had worked for us.

I also visited the wounded Yechiel, whose life had miraculously been spared. He was in the Kaplan Hospital, which had been temporarily converted to a military hospital. Dark bodies rested on the white sheets, many of them young men from the new immigration, from the Eastern countries.

Studies in school got underway only a few days before Hannukkah.

The first rains of that winter fell on a Sabbath, in the evening. The next day I arrived at the school early, in order to make the necessary arrangements for a rainy day. Mordecai had left for Tel Aviv before dawn. The streets were completely empty. Suddenly I heard screams, in a woman's voice. I looked around, but saw no one. The screams grew louder, and I ran in the direction of the cries. When I reached the spot, I saw that the cries were coming from a pickup truck that stood beside our clinic. They were the cries of a woman from Sdeh-David, who was in labour and had been brought to the village centre in order to be taken to the hospital in an ambulance. But at that hour — Sunday morning — neither ambulance, doctor, nor nurse were in the village. A single nurse remained on duty on the Sabbath to serve three villages. That morning she had been taken in the ambulance to give emergency treatment to the victim of an accident in Noga.

The driver wanted to go and bring the nurse, but the car refused to start. The driver left the couple in the pickup truck and started for Noga on foot. Meanwhile, the woman's labour pains grew harder. The confused husband left his wife and ran after the driver, to tell him to hurry. The woman grew frightened and attempted to get out of the car, but for some reason the door would not open, and she grew even more terrified...

I opened the door of the car and freed the 'prisoner'. She was a young woman with a delicate face and long hair. In her bewilderment, she clung to me and cried: "I'm ready! I'm ready!"

I grasped the fact that she did not know Hebrew, and wanted to say that she was giving birth. I also began to shout. At the sound one of the women of Nehora came running, still in her nightgown. There was no longer any need for an ambulance: by this time, the young woman simply needed a bed, so that she wouldn't give birth in the street, in the rain.

We made a "seat" for her with crossed arms, and with great effort got her into my house, and put her to bed in my bed. A moment later, I lifted into the air by its tiny legs the precious loot — a newborn baby. Its body was blue, its face twisted with crying, and the umbilical cord was still attached.

The young mother was suffering more from embarrassment than pain. She kissed both of us continually, and begged our pardon for the trouble she had caused us. I myself was enormously happy that a living being had been born in my bed, as though I were a partner in the enterprise.

A few minutes later the nurse, the husband, and the ambulance driver appeared in our house. We wrapped the baby in diapers that the mother had brought with her on her way to the hospital, put the mother on a real stretcher, and sent her together with her little daughter for a "vacation" in the hospital.

The embarrassed husband wanted to help me clean up the house. I would not allow it, and said to him: "For me it's a great honour — don't take it away from me! We'll do better to drink to the health of your new daughter."

Over a glass of wine the father, an immigrant from Tunis,

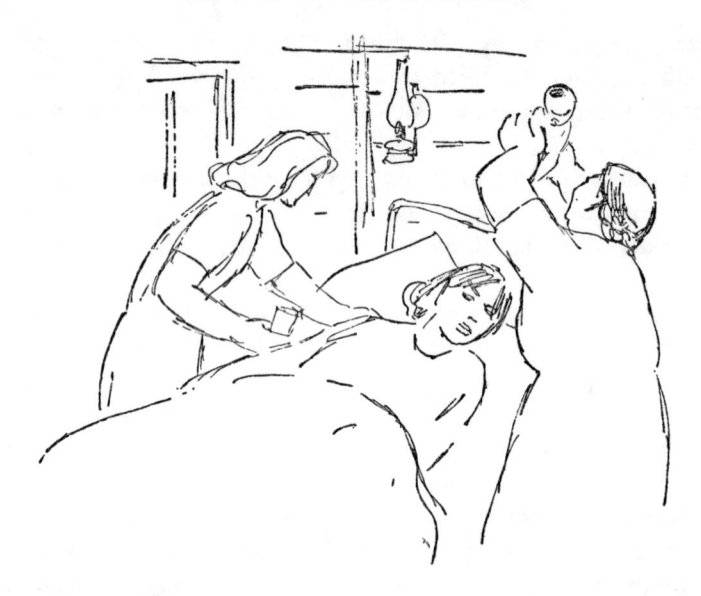

told me that the baby was the sixth to be born in his family, and the eldest was already eight years old. He was hard put to support a family of eight. He was lucky that his wife was a good, industrious worker. She worked unceasingly from morning till late at night, so their house would be clean and the children would grow up well. Indeed, "A heavy burden is a pleasant burden."

The man added: "We'll name the child after you."

"No," I replied. "I've got a better name for her. Have you heard about our chief of staff, the hero of the Sinai Campaign, Moshe Dayan?"

"Of course I have." The man was astonished. "What do you suggest, that we call the little girl 'Dayana'?"

"No," I said. "Let her bear the name of a woman who did not live to see these great days. She died a short time before the Sinai Campaign. She took a great part in that campaign, although no one knows about it except the chief of staff himself, for she was his mother."

And so the little girl's name in Israel is — Devorah.

Only for my young neighbour Carmela was the Sinai Campaign not yet over: Her husband Menachem was still halfway around the world aboard a frigate. She waited impatiently for news, and all of us felt rather guilty in her presence.

One day one of the team of workers from Nehora came back from Migdal and informed us that he had heard a news broadcast that morning, and there was an announcement that the frigate had reached the port of Eilat safely and the entire crew would be flown to their homes.

The bell rang for the beginning of classes, and the children all went into their classrooms. I was sitting at my table in the teachers' room, absorbed in my work. Suddenly I heard gay voices, and Carmela and Menachem appeared before me, together with everyone they had met along the way.

I rang the school bell energetically and stopped the lessons in the middle. When everyone had grown a little calmer and the cheering that greeted Menachem died down, we invited him, his wife, and his little son to one of the classrooms where we assembled the older pupils. Holding his son in one arm, Menachem sketched a map of Africa on the blackboard, marked the route of the frigate around Africa in coloured chalk, and explained the object of the operation to the pupils.

In the evening, at a party for friends and acquaintances from the centre and from the villages, Menachem told us the story of his two-month voyage. He gave presents to all his friends and told us about the natives of the dark continent, whom he had met when the frigate anchored in the port of Djibouti.

What impressed us most was the description of the traditional ceremony of presentation of the Order of Knighthood of the Sea God, Neptune, which took place when the frigate crossed the equator. Every sailor who crosses the equator for the first time gets a ducking in a barrel full of machine oil. He is then rolled in flour and tar, and is finally given rum to drink from a goblet that holds an entire bottle. After this, the poor sailor, who now looks like a scarecrow, is given an honorary certificate from the god Neptune, which frees him from the threat of similar ordeals for the rest of his life.

Naturally, Menachem guards this document as the apple of his eye...

XXI

ELECTRICITY FOR THE VILLAGES

While we were still living in Noga, plans were drawn up for connecting the villages of the Lachish region to the national power network of the Electric Company. The settlers in the new region were still burdened with the necessity of standing guard duty at night, in addition to their farm work. The army also did its share in protecting these villages. When night fell, traffic on the highway stopped; but after a week or two of quiet, people would begin to leave the villages briefly in the evenings. One night I went to Ashkelon with Mordecai in the car—a quarter of an hour's drive. Between the two sections of the city, the old and the new, there was an uninhabited stretch of about two kilometres. As we approached the new Ashkelon, we heard a tremendous explosion behind us. The crowd strolling on the outskirts of the town became panicky. Military police arrived at once, and we learned that the car immediately behind us had run onto a mine and two of its occupants had been killed on the spot.

Clashes with infiltrators were daily occurrences. Almost every night horses or sheep were stolen from the villages, and we were used to being awakened by shots. The settlers were afraid to get together in the evenings for celebrations, for they remembered the tragic lesson of the wedding of the village of Patish, where a grenade had been thrown into a circle of dancers by infiltrators who penetrated into the village, twenty kilometres from the border.

Standing watch in the villages was made far more difficult by the lack of electric lighting in the area. The settlers pleaded for electricity and lighting, even from a generator, such as was given to border settlements. However, the authorities claimed that the expense was not justified. The first villages in the Lachish region were built in the section bordering the coastal plain, through which the national power network passes. In the opinion of the authorities, it would be far better to connect the villages to the national network than to bring in generators.

The Sinai campaign proved the justice of our claims, and as soon as the campaign was over, electric poles were set up, high tension lines were brought in, and everything was made ready for connecting the power lines to the houses.

But at the last minute, the work stopped; experts from the Electric Company had examined the houses and found a flaw in construction that prevented connecting the houses to the power line: a certain insulation was lacking in the roofs of the houses, and if electricity were connected, the houses would be dangerous during the rainy season. The frames of the roofs were poured concrete and it was impossible to drive a nail into them. In order to extract the electric pipes from the walls of the house and make the required repair on them, it would be necessary — according to the experts from the Electric Company — to break through the concrete, and afterwards to repair the break. "Solel Boneh" would take a loss, after this repair, of IL 35 per house for every house in the region. The houses were uniform, and the flaw in construction was also uniform: it was reproduced hundreds of times. All construction work in the settlements of Otsem, Noga, Shakhar, and Zohar had already been completed when the flaw was discovered. In Nehora, however, whose houses had been constructed at a later date, and in Nir-Khen, which had also been built after the other settlements in the region, the error was not made, so there was no delay in connecting these two settlements to the power line.

Nir-Khen is a *moshav-shitufi* (a cooperative settlement, which is administered as one large farm, although every family has its own house, and the families receive salaries). It was founded by a group of Israeli youth from Haifa. The settlement was founded in 1955, when Ben-Gurion called on the youth of the country to settle in the Negev. The group was allotted 5,000 dunams of fertile land, and an unlimited quantity of water. The name "Nir-Khen" was adopted in memory of the 58 Israelis who perished in the "El-Al" passenger plane which was shot down over Bulgaria.

In the group were forty members, some of them married, who refused to move their families into the temporary huts in which the other residents of the area had lived until shortly before the Sinai Campaign. The Settlement Department used their own weapon against them: first priority for building was given to the villages where the settlers had been living in huts together with their children and elderly parents since 1955. In Nir-Khen, therefore, the temporary huts so typical of the region's settlements were never erected; its houses were built last, as were those of Nehora, and for this reason their houses did not contain the flaw in construction that was discovered in the houses of the other villages.

From the beginning it was hard to adapt the village centre to its functions. Contradictions became apparent. The fact that the people who held jobs of a supervisory nature lived outside the villages they served created a kind of "privileged class" in the region, and could easily produce feelings of inferiority and suspicions of discrimination on the part of the settlers in the villages.

There were also other disappointments: the attraction the village centre had for intellectual workers was far less than desirable, and candidates with suitable professional backgrounds were lacking, especially in the branches of teaching and medicine.

The settlers of the villages came to Lachish as *immigrants*. They settled in Otsem, Shakhar and Noga, and built their permanent homes. In contrast, most of the residents of the village centre appeared to be "emigrants", who had moved there because of economic advantages, and who would be ready to move back to the city at the first opportune moment.

We were much distressed by the hindrance that postponed the connection of electricity to the first villages of Lachish. Negotiations over this matter were prolonged and wearisome. "Solel Boneh" and the Electric Company carried on a lengthy debate over the question of who should bear the losses caused by the flaw in the construction of the houses, which prevented their immediately being connected to the power line.

We regarded electricity as the most important factor for rapid development of the village centre. The clinic needed electricity so that the walls would not be blackened by the smoke of the kerosene camp stove on which the hypodermics were sterilized. The preservation of expensive medicines required constant refrigeration. The residents needed an occasional showing of a film. Electricity was also needed for evening classes, for the regular operation of the library, and for the tractor station, which needed electric welding.

We were convinced that it was necessary to create a public consciousness of public needs being more important than private needs. With this in mind, electricity was first supplied to the public institutions of the village centre. But we did not realize that the Electric Company would not agree to send its technicians to Nehora a second time in order to connect the electricity to the private houses. The Company's representatives claimed that many villages in all sections of the country had been waiting their turns for some time to receive electricity, and an orderly work schedule did not permit the Company to connect the electricity in a village only in part.

We dreaded the moment when the lights would go on in the houses of the "ruling class" of Nehora. In private conversation, several residents of the centre admitted to me that they felt uncomfortable at receiving electricity before people who had preceded them in settling in Lachish, and thanks to whom the region had been redeemed. But it was beyond my powers to convince most of Nehora's residents of the justice of this claim. All of them put fuses in their fuse-boxes, and there was light in Nehora.

The light of a kerosene lamp continued to flicker in our house, and this small detail blunted, to some degree, the sting of bitterness and the complaints of the settlers in the neighbouring villages, who visited us frequently at that time, especially in the evenings.

"Why don't you turn on the electric light?" they often asked us.

"Because the time hasn't come for it yet."

"And when will the time come?"

"Not until your turn comes."

No one knew how long the debate between the Electric Company and "Solel Boneh" over who would bear the expense of the repairs would go on. Winter passed, and we were well into spring. As we were making preparations for the Festival of First Fruits, when the settlers were to bring their produce to the village centre for the first time, one of the children of Noga spoke to me.

"Teacher," he said. "We aren't going to have a Festival! Our parents say we're going to have a strike, because they've given Nir-Khen electricity..."

At first, I paid no attention to the child's words, which I thought were without foundation. However, that same night one of the watchmen, also a resident of Noga, came to our house and asked me to step outside with him. Without a word, he pointed in the direction of Nir-Khen.

I was shocked at seeing the electric lights flooding the settlement of Israeli youth, which had taken upon itself to darken, with its light, all the neighbouring villages — the settlements of cave dwellers, North Africans and Kurds, who were left in the darkness.

I had never before experienced such a moment — such a

feeling of complete worthlessness, lack of the slightest influence, of utter failure in education. I demanded of Mordecai that he take me away from Lachish at once, to wherever he wanted to go. We were bankrupt here, and we no longer had any justification for our existence in this place. For eight months we had deceived these naive people, we had preached patience and they had believed that there was someone who would see to it that they were not discriminated against...

Since that unforgettable night and the time I am writing this, the incident of "Wadi Salib" occurred*, a shameful incident in the nation's history. At the time Nir-Khen pushed to the head of the line and took extra privileges for itself, the concept of "Wadi Salib" had not yet crystallized, but I sensed it in the tense atmosphere of the villages in Lachish which had been left without electric light. I sensed it in the encouragement with which our driver from Noga parted from me in Rechovot, on the night I left Lachish. He kissed my hands when I said to him: "We are to blame for this wrong. If it is not corrected, I won't come back."

In the morning I travelled with Mordecai from Rechovot to Tel Aviv, to one of the engineers of the Jewish Agency. We told him about the situation that had been created, which we regarded as being most serious. There was high tension among the settlers in the villages of Lachish, and anything might happen.

---

* Riots in Haifa caused by ostensible discrimination against immigrants from eastern communities.

The settlers did not forget the affair, even two years after electricity had been installed throughout the entire Lachish region. During the elections for the fourth Knesset, when a violent verbal war was being waged among the various parties, and the differences between the two main communities — Ashkenazi and Sephardic — were being emphasized, especially in the areas settled by new immigrants, we were sitting in the house of Rivka Ben-Tolila and discussing the affairs of the day with her clever, intelligent sons.

One of them burst out tauntingly: "And why did you give electricity to Nir-Khen out of turn?"

I felt as though I had been scalded. "Khalfon, how can you?..."

"With all due respect, just the same you failed!"

And, indeed, he was right...

The Agency engineer did not know what advice to give us: on the one hand, you had to admit... and on the other hand, you couldn't forget... And what could you do? Our "boys" in Nir-Khen are clever and sharp. They had gotten tired of waiting for the electricity to be connected to all the villages. And as they knew how to deal with all the authorities, they had paid the required sum to the Electric Company and had received electricity. And what could we do to them now? The law protecting consumers prevents anything being done about it...

Mordecai told me that he must return to Lachish: the head of the council was responsible for whatever happened in his area. I stayed in the city to do everything possible to prevent its being claimed that electricity in Lachish was distributed by "race". No one had intentionally done this, but the existing state of affairs hit one in the eye, so to speak. There are two thinly-populated settlements in the Lachish region — Nehora and Nir-Khen, both of which are populated almost entirely by Ashkenazim — in the heart of an entire region which is, more or less, the territory of Eastern — or Sephardic — communities. What would we teach them, and where would we lead them? Was this the way?

In the morning I went to the main office of the Electric Company and requested an appointment with the chief administrator. I talked to him for two hours. He was very sorry, but he saw no way to correct the wrong. Nothing illegal had been done, he claimed — Nir-Khen had made payment and received electricity in a legal manner.

I explained to him that something illegal had been done by the area administration: it had not understood the matter when it gave orders for the electricity to be connected in Nehora in the beginning, and the results might well be grave for the entire area. The settlers of the villages, who had not hesitated to organize strikes and start riots at the least suspicion of favouritism on the part of the "authorities in charge", certainly would not keep silent when the "privileged class" and the "Vus-vusim"* had managed to obtain such an important benefit for themselves...

The administrator promised to send a letter to "Solel Boneh" concerning the immediate repair of the roofs in the villages, and to inform us at once of the reply, when he received it.

"I'll wait here while you write it," I said. "And I'll take it to "Solel Boneh" myself, so there won't be any new red tape."

He was astonished. "But you're only making unnecessary work for yourself."

"That's all right — time is more precious than gold..."

When I received the letter, I hurried to the offices of "Solel Boneh", where I was told that they would have to consult with representatives of the Agency. That day I took a number of letters from office to office, like a postal messenger. I went to the Agency, and from there back to the other offices. It grew late, and the offices were about to close. I had to postpone

---

* A mocking term for Ashkenazim.

the matter till the next day. Next morning I returned to the offices of "Solel Boneh" and succeeded in getting into a meeting of representatives of the three bodies concerned. They sat and discussed how to repair simultaneously the roofs in all four villages.

One of the engineers suggested a way to connect the electricity in all the villages immediately. The rains would start only in another four months. The roofs would be repaired individually, one after the other, and each house under repair would be separately disconnected, and then reconnected. The work would be finished before the rainy season began.

Here began the process of signing contracts, which I know nothing about. I was forced to seek Mordecai's advice. I went to Ashkelon and phoned him to come and meet me. When he heard what I had to say, Mordecai promised to send the four instructors of the four villages to Tel Aviv the next day with the required sum of money for signing the contracts.

Afterwards I returned to Rechovot and went to see the engineer of the Electric Company, an old acquaintance of ours, who would be responsible for carrying out the work. I asked him to schedule a crew of electricians to go to Lachish the next morning as soon as the contracts were signed.

Apparently word had already reached him about the troubles I had been making for the Electric Company. The engineer looked at me suspiciously, as though I were not quite right in my mind, and spoke to me in the pacifying tone that parents use to a spoiled child when there are guests in the house.

"Everything is going to be all right! You don't need to worry any more. Is this your affair? Come, get into my car, and I'll take you home..."

I thanked him with all my heart, but I refused to go home without the workers from the Electric Company.

An engineer named Laor, a resident of Ramat-Gan, drove

the pickup truck that took the workers to Lachish. I sat beside him and was forced to listen to his angry words. He was enraged: his crew had been taken off work in a village that had been waiting patiently for electricity for more than five years. A woman like me shook people's faith in the nation's official bodies. Everything here is accomplished only through "*proteksia*"...

I was worn out from the events of the last few days and from the complicated affairs with which I had been dealing, for which there was no precedent in my life. The man who sat beside me seemed to be an honest, decent man, but I did not have the strength to explain to him and try to convince him. I only nodded my head in agreement with all his terms of reproach, and said:

"You're absolutely right."

When we reached Noga, the engineer asked me, "Where should we start making the connections?"

"In the synagogue," I replied.

I went into the nearest house and asked for a kerchief to cover my head. When I had seen the first electric light burning inside the synagogue I walked home to Nehora.

XXII

LAKE ZOHAR

"A lifted goblet of skyblue wine is Lake Zohar —
made by man, it is pleasant in the landscape."
Shin Shalom, "*Lachish*"

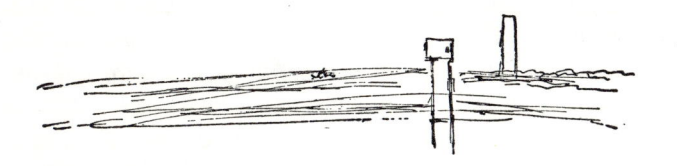

LACHISH RECEIVED another gift after the Sinai Campaign, one even more important to farmers than electric light — Lake Zohar. The work was begun in May, 1957, and in the winter of the same year the waters of the Yarkon River flowed into the giant reservoir that holds 8.5 million cubic metres of water. As it is written: "*He turneth the wilderness into a pool of water.*"

The source of the fresh water that irrigates and sustains the new region is quite distant: it comes to us from Rosh Ha'ayin, near Petakh Tiqva. Before the lake existed, during the Sinai Campaign, our main prayer was that nothing should happen to the pipeline. Now we have an artificial lake in the heart of the area. With this "giant's goblet", there is no fear of explosions or sabotage. The water in Lake Zohar is not only water for security, but water for saving, a kind of "water bank". The lake fills in the winter months, when water consumption is reduced and the runoff waters of the Yarkon are plentiful. The water reserves are used in the summer, when water consumption reaches a peak and the Yarkon cannot supply the entire consumption.

This giant project can be expressed in a column of large figures: a million and a quarter cubic metres of earth moved: a million tons of stone brought in to reinforce the embankments, which are four metres wide, and on which you can walk completely around the lake; a circumference which is more than two and a half kilometres long. The lake permits irrigation of an additional 30,000 dunams per year — an area cultivated in cotton, peanuts, potatoes, and other crops. Without the lake, this land would have remained barren. The project cost the government four million pounds, but the great benefits it has given us justify the expense.

During the eight months in which the lake was being excavated, it was the principal subject of our conversation. We marvelled at it, as though it were a rocket to the moon. Pessimists cast doubt on the success of the project and predicted failure, for past experience with large reservoirs in Israel had not been encouraging. The chances of successfully preventing absorption of the water into the floor of the artificial lake were slim.

However, Tahel made the plan, and Mekorot attacked the job, astonishing the inhabitants of Lachish by the feverish pace of work. Overnight hundreds of workers and an army of heavy machinery of various kinds appeared in our region, including giant machines the like of which had never before been seen in the country. To the spoken tongue were added new names: "Marion", "Euclid." These were not the names of film stars: Marion was the name of the "beauty" who grasped tens of cubic metres of earth in her steel fingers and filled a truck with it in a matter of seconds, and the Euclid would haul the huge load and pour it along the sides of the dam, until the retaining walls rose to a height of 21 metres.

These stupendous machines moved like strange, prehistoric animals. They gouged out whole mountains with their beaks, almost seeming to change the laws of the first creation. Tens of tractors, steam shovels, streamrollers and trucks formed a kind of moving production line. A hundred and twenty men worked in two shifts, and the work area recalled the overthrow of Sodom in its day.

A restaurant was set up in Nehora for the men working on the lake. Anyone who entered it during the lunch hour would be confronted with peculiar creatures, not to be encountered in any other spot: workers covered from head to foot with plaster and slime, and smeared with oil — creatures with almost no resemblance to human beings.

The most important work went into the construction of the lake floor, in order to prevent leakage and loss of water. The lake floor was covered with a layer of clay six metres thick. The layer of clay was watered every day, and afterwards packed down with steam-rollers. This operation was repeated numerous times until the clay was pressed into a hard layer. When the water of the Yarkon first flowed into the new lake, the clay bottom absorbed the water to saturation point, though at a very slow rate. The upper layer, to a depth of a metre and a half, turned into a clay bog, like the large and extremely dangerous swamps in the forests of Polesia in Poland. This layer of bog is the best guarantee against leakage of water.

Lake Zohar is surrounded by a high barbed-wire fence, and its gates are closed, locked and bolted. Around the fence are warning signs with inscriptions in several languages: "Entrance Into Enclosed Area Is Absolutely Prohibited! Trespassers Will Be Punished!"

Why is trespassing such a grave offence? Because the quiet waters of the artificial lake hold great danger. Anyone who goes into the lake is risking his life. The teachers repeated this time and again to their pupils, but all their warnings did not lessen the attraction of the lake, which entranced the children and young people during the burning days of summer — until an accident occurred that gave a tragic demonstration of the lake's dangers. The boat of the lake watchman overturned, and although he was an excellent swimmer, he was trapped by the treacherous clay bog and was unable to free himself. A crew of navy divers was called in, and they laboured for four days in search of his body.

The gate of the lake was opened, of course, for tourists and visitors. Whoever gets through the gate and goes up onto the retaining wall sees a magnificent scene. The lake is huge and blue, and at its foot lies the entire region: the villages of Lachish, the city of Kiryat-Gat, and in the distance — the mountains of Hebron. Below the lake stretch broad fields of cotton, dark green in the middle of summer, and white as snow at the beginning of fall.

We were interested in learning what impression our lake made on others. If they compared it to the Kinneret, we would comment:

"Lake Zohar isn't like the Kinneret. The Kinneret can be seen from a distance, from every hill in the surrounding countryside. This isn't true of our lake. Our lake is on *top* of a hill, 117 metres above sea level. The water irrigates the fields of Lachish by gravity. Lake Zohar can't be seen from below at all. And the main thing is that Lake Kinneret has existed since the first days of creation, while Lake Zohar is a completely *new* lake, and the work of man..."

On the great day when the President opened the "faucet" that fills the lake (at a distance of six kilometres away), the harbor engineer Yaakov Levin stood on the retaining wall and, in a ceremony attended by cabinet ministers and numerous distinguished guests, officially announced the existence of a new lake in Israel. On that day we brought all the children of the regional school to see the first water flowing into Lake Zohar. But before the great moment arrived, we took the children and walked across the floor of the lake, from bank to bank, and we told them:

"Remember, children, and don't forget! When you are old, you can tell your grandchildren: 'When I was a child, I walked across our lake on dry land!'..."

XXIII

INVESTMENTS IN THE SPIRIT

WATER WAS NOT the only vital necessity we stored up for ourselves in the region of Lachish. In our two public libraries — the central library in Nehora, named after Dr. Ben-Zion Gat (a teacher in the Rechavia High School in Jerusalem, and one of the founders of "The President's Fund For Immigrant Children"), and the municipal library in Kiryat Gat, named after Rivka Alper (an author who wrote about the achievements of the country's first pioneers) — we already have ten thousand books and five hundred regular readers, most of them children and young people.

Not one of us knew how to ensure lasting achievements, or how to go about creating *habits* of reading. We made 'investments in the Spirit' as we made investments in farm implements and technical equipment. We stood helplessly facing the huge number of illiterates in our area. When we succeeded in teaching a young man or woman how to read and write, we rejoiced — as though this accomplishment had instantly wiped out all their ignorance...

For more than ten years the nation's cultural bodies have been struggling to bring the book into development areas. The Department of Education and the Centre for Culture tried distributing libraries to the new immigrant settlements. Several years ago I was sent to inspect these libraries. In part they were locked away and closed, like "dead souls", and in part they were broken open and scattered. In a cupboard without a lock could be found a few volumes of books, a large number of propaganda pamphlets, and a multitude of filing cards. These cards were for the use of the local youth instructors who had completed a brief course in library work at the Histadrut school in Bet Berl. Here are examples of several cards I found:

Title of Book: Isaiah
Author: A. A. Akavia
Title of Book: Psalms
Author: A. A. Akavia

In this particular catalogue, it seemed that the talented author, A.A. Akavia (the name of the distinguished commentator, incidentally), had "written" the books of Ezekiel, Job, Genesis, and the five scrolls!...

I tried to discuss the matter with the young man who "passed the course" in Bet Berl, but he disagreed violently and tried to convince me that this was in complete accordance with what he had been taught — to look for the name of the author on the title page, and never to deviate from that principle.

Once I sent a friend of mine a book for her grandson, a pupil in second grade. It was the story of "The Fisherman and the Fish of Gold" by Pushkin. My friend wrote me: "Pushkin is still Pushkin: the children still love the old fisherman, hate his old wife, and justify the fish."

I thought to myself: when will the Kurdish child of seven identify himself with heroes whose acquaintance he has made in a book? This is not simply a technical ability; in the words of John Dewey — *Reading is also a process that is closely connected with thinking and the solution of problems, and understanding the contents of what is read is an active and constructive spiritual process.* There is no higher educational goal than that of teaching the pupil good reading habits and how to understand the contents of what he reads.

I received a peculiar enjoyment from one of the truants whom I once found behind the schoolhouse. He sat there reading utterly absorbed in his book. When I drew near and he finally noticed me, he was stricken with alarm. He was holding the sixth volume of "Captain Grant's Children". This was one of the boys from Noga, a pupil in the eighth grade. The vocabulary of his mother, with whom I was acquainted, was no more than a hundred words.

I remarked to the boy that in my childhood, I too had occasionally skipped a lesson because of an interesting book, but that all the same, a teacher had to be strict in cases like this. He smiled and went back to his classroom.

When I was still in Noga, I invited the teacher from Jerusalem, Miriam Carmon, to a 'Sabbath Welcome' at school. She told the pupils about the siege of Jerusalem in the War of Independence, and about the part the children played in the defence of the city. She spoke in a quiet voice, but her young listeners grew very excited and one of them asked:

"You saw all that yourself? It really happened? Did they *write* about it in a *book?*"

As the Biblical verse has it: "*To teach the sons of Judah the bow. Behold, it is written in the book of Jashar.*"...

Friday is the day most books are borrowed from the library: the children receive "a book for the Sabbath". The chatter of the children telling one another about different books and advising their friends to borrow "a terrific book" — when the actual merits of the book barely matter; the angry "I asked for it first!"; the brightened eyes of a tiny scholar intoxicated by his chance discovery of a good book — these things refresh the heart no less than the green fields that surround the villages of Lachish.

> *Currents of enlightening letters*
> *Washed over them like waves,*
> *Spurted into their thirsting mouths*
> *Slaking their thirst with knowledge.*

— Z. Shneur, "The Miracle of Gutenburg"
Meanwhile, how few were the thirsting mouths!...

Near the David Shimoni regional school surrounded by a well-kept garden, stands a house already shaded by trees. Beside the front door is a shining plaque with this inscription:

"The Hebrew Author's Guild, the Dvorah Barron Guest House for Authors and Artists."

Many people ask: "What good does this house do you, and who comes to visit in this isolated corner?"

Our intention was not to receive favours from them, but to *give* the nation's artists and writers a share in the new Lachish, and we wanted our children to have respect for men of knowledge, and to show courtesy to scholars and creative artists. The very fact of their spending some time among us can both draw them closer to us and give us the benefit of their spiritual influence.

"*Let us make, I pray thee, a little chamber on the roof; and let us set for him there a bed, and a table, and a stool, and a candlestick; and it shall be, when he cometh to us, that he shall turn in thither.*" (Kings II, 4, 10)

Among our guests were Shmuel and Henya Yavnieli, a couple from the Second Aliya. As was our custom before the scheduled arrival of an author at the guest house, we told the pupils about the man and his work. Once we read them several chapters from Yavnieli's *A Trip to Yemen*. During his visit, there was a general meeting of all the parents in the region to hear a lecture by Israel Yeshiahu, who was born in Yemen.

When I welcomed him, I told him: "You can't imagine who you're going to meet at your lecture. You'll have a marvellous illustration for your talk on the value and power of education."

That evening I took the Yavnieli couple to the hall, which was already filled with people. And, indeed, Israel Yeshiahu was enormously surprised. Greatly excited, he told the audience of immigrants how Yavnieli had brought the news of the establishment of the state of Israel to Yemen, and what a great part he had played in bringing that community to Israel and in aiding their adjustment to their new life here. The impressive experience ended with the recital of Natan Alterman's poem, *Second Aliyah,* by one of the children of Noga:

Today they go through the country and see
Workshops and gardens and fruitful fields,
Farmers, labourers, Hebrew soldiers
Villages, settlements, Hebrew towns.

They say: A nation of farmers and builders —
Who would have dreamed it? How times have changed!

And those who see them
Say about them:
What peculiar people!
It's all so simple ...
What is there to wonder at, or marvel?
Really, what very peculiar people!

Anyone who has never seen Shmuel and Henya Yavnieli, filled with excitement and exclaiming over things that are no more than the end results of projects implemented by their own generation fifty years ago, has never really seen "peculiar people"!...

Another unexpected and exciting meeting occurred in the Dvorah Barron House between the Hebrew writer and educator from the United States, Professor Zvi Sharfstein, and a teacher of Hebrew from India, whose dark face was wreathed in a white beard.

In the village of Shakhar live ten families of immigrants from Cochin, who form a unique collective. On one of my visits to Shakhar, the elder from Cochin, Reb Shlomo Eliahu, asked me:

"Do you know a Professor Srafastein from America?"

"Professor Sharfstein is in the country now — but how do you know him?" I asked in astonishment.

The scholar from Cochin had taught Torah and the Hebrew language in the city of Perure in Travangore, one of the Indian states, for over thirty years. Throughout the years he had exchanged letters with Professor Sharfstein, and from him had received letters of instruction, textbooks for the pupils and supplementary texts for the teachers. The American professor had cast his bread upon the waters, and for tens of years his admirer in India had faithfully followed his activities in the field of Hebrew education, even saving newspapers in which his name was mentioned.

When Professor Sharfstein and his wife came to the Dvorah Barron House, he went to Shakhar to visit his long-time friend, whom he had never met in person. On the Sabbath, Shlomo, Eliahu and his family came to Nehora to return the visit.

Across the table the two scholars of East and West carried on their discussion while the young people sat listening in awe, with the characteristic courtesy of this Jewish tribe.

The scene was a striking one, owing to the emphatic contrast between them: their completely different cast of features, and the utter lack of any racial resemblance whatsoever between the two. Nevertheless, it was obvious that they were closely attached to each other. The Hebrew teacher from the United States showed an active concern for the education of the children of the Jews of India. Their common language was Hebrew; and the vision — the return to Zion.

The poet, Hannania Reichman, wrote a poem on the occasion of the first trees being planted in the Lachish region. Ever since, the poem has been recited every year in the Tu-b'Shvat (Arbor Day) program put on by the school-children. They have already repeated the program several times, and every schoolchild in Lachish knows the poem by heart. Once, when I had gone for a walk with Hannania Reichman, we met some children. I introduced him to them.

"Ah, he's the *Gateway to the Negev!*" said one of the children, referring to the opening words of the poem:

Gateway to the Negev is Lachish,
For two thousand years it was waste and still ...

The guest house in Nehora also has "permanent residents" who come back year after year. They are looked upon as distinguished guests in Lachish, and they have great influence. They have made friends among both children and adults, who miss them and await their arrival.

One of these is Shin Shalom. When he comes to Nehora,

numbers of settlers come to visit him and invite him to their homes. When he goes out for a stroll in the countryside, the settlers in the other villages also greet him with affection and respect, for his poetry is well-known to them. In school they study his poetry, devote a "program" to Shin Shalom, bring him flowers, and learn that they who give are they who receive.

One winter night Shin Shalom lingered in our house. The conversation dealt with the problems of the villages, the effect of the passing of time and the effects of uprooting people from their native soil. Suddenly the door opened unexpectedly, and a young woman came into the room. She was crying bitterly, and her words were so indistinct that it was impossible to understand what had happened. When she grew somewhat calmer and stopped crying, I gathered from what she said that her husband was threatening to drive her out of the house.

She was still telling me the story of her troubles when the door opened a second time and her father-in-law and her husband appeared. The old man announced that he had decided to send his son to the rabbi the next day to divorce his wife, because people were gossiping about her and saying that she was having an "affair" with the neighbour...

We heard the report with astonishment: the neighbour of whom they spoke was an elderly man, a father and grandfather many times over, whose own wife was still regularly presenting him with offspring. We were still pondering over this odd affair when the door opened a third time, and the woman's neighbour entered the room together with his wife, who was pregnant, and their son, a pupil in the eighth grade.

All of them began to shout at the top of their lungs, and a fist fight seemed practically inevitable. Over the years we had become accustomed to "differences of opinion" of this kind. But the affair made a terrible impression on the sensitive poet. He tried to reconcile the two sides, pleading with each of them in turn. Mordecai investigated the reason for the dispute, and discovered that the husband's father demanded that his daughter-in-law "not be talked about."

All our powers of persuasion and explanation did not succeed in convincing him that the woman herself was powerless to stop the tongues of gossipers.

Shin Shalom was incapable of dismissing the matter from his thoughts, and he persisted in his efforts to reconcile the two sides. He preached them a sermon:

"Things like this happen among you because of your lack of education and the lack of books in your home. What? They don't know how to read? But here's the boy, he knows. You ought to sit with your parents on the Sabbath and read them the weekly portion..."

The boy was the only one of them all who remained silent. It was heart-rending to see him trapped in this uproar. His father had brought him in order to demonstrate the inequality of the two sides: his young son as opposed to the grown son of his opponent.

Mordecai finally got tired of listening to the shouts and curses and suggested that the two sides sign a "non-aggression contract." As an old hand in drawing up contracts, Mordecai wrote out a contract on the spot in which each side agreed to stay "fed up" with the other, meaning that neither would go through his neighbour's yard, neither would say 'Shalom' to the other, and neither would speak either a good or evil word about the other.

Mordecai read the "contract" to them, and after several minor changes of expression, the two sides reached an agreement. Mordecai then handed his guests the stamp pad, and each of them pressed his thumb on it and "signed" the contract. Shin Shalom also wished to have the honour of signing the "peace treaty", and therefore we have a uniquely autographed document: an agreement to a promise "not to speak", signed with the thumbprints of the disputants, and witnessed with the well-known signature of the poet, Shin Shalom...

And what metamorphosis did the chaos of the early days of Lachish undergo in the poet's soul?

> *You took pity on me in the smoke and the soot*
> *Of a turbulent city of discord and strife —*
> *In the village, at rest, I am one with the secret*
> *Of night's page now ended, and day's just begun*
> *And the morn rolling back from the plain, to pour forth*
> *Sweet scents of the day the Messiah will come.*
> — Shin Shalom 'Lachish'

Another regular visitor to the Dvorah Barron House was the aging author Moshe Stavi, a former member of the old Beer Tuvia, in its first settlement, fifty years ago. People living in the South know him well. He was a farmer for many years, and most of his writings are devoted to the soil and the men who till it. In his books he described the old Beer Tuvia. He had an unusual understanding of animals and he writes about them in his book of stories *Dumb Friends*. He described his encounters with the Arab *fellahin* over several decades in his book, *The Arab Village*.

To this day, on the anniversary of the founding of Beer Tuvia the children recite the poem of comfort written by Moshe Stavi for the looted Beer Tuvia, which was razed to the ground by its Arab neighbours in the riots of 1929. The author-farmer was shaken by the sight of the ruin, which he described in a touching lament, and he goes on to prophesy the revival of Beer Tuvia and its flowering anew. This comforting prophecy has been completely fulfilled.

Times have changed now. Today few adults care about understanding animals, or take an interest in poetry about tillers of the soil of earlier periods of immigration: but his young readers are loyal to Stavi, especially those from the immigrant settlements. His tales of the East, collected in a large volume of marvellous stories, filled with truth and the wisdom of experience, are wellknown to the children of Lachish.

The settlers in the villages of Lachish have a special respect for this author both for his venerable age and his strong figure, for his knowledge of the Arabic language, for his own respect for the customs and ways of life of the peoples of the East, for his intelligence and the hidden treasure of folk proverbs and parables with which he spices his speech. Moshe Stavi is hot-tempered, always ready to argue hotly over matters concerning the language, nature and farming, which he knows so thoroughly.

As was our custom in the school in Nehora, the pupils invited the distinguished guest to one of the 'Sabbath Welcomes'. When Stavi was asked to tell the pupils a story, he told them his recollections of his first days in the country:

"... I had a letter to a young man in Kibbutz Tel-Khai. I went to the kibbutz. They told me he was out in the field. I went there and found him and another two men loading sheaves of wheat onto a high wagon with 'ladder' sides. Three were down below, pitching the sheaves onto the wagon with pitchforks, while on the wagon stood a single man, who was expertly arranging the sheaves in heaps with his one hand. When he finished loading the one-armed man drove off, and we walked back to the kibbutz on foot.

"When we reached the kibbutz, we seated ourselves at the dining-table to eat dinner. I heard the one-armed man, who was nicknamed 'Osiya', talking rapidly, mainly in Russian. Osiya urged me to eat, and kept pushing my plate towards me.

"As for me, I felt as though my throat had been sealed up! I thought to myself how the very food on my plate was indebted to the toil of the one-armed man. I had seen with my own eyes what a hard worker he was — the man who afterwards became known by everyone as Yosef Trumpeldor. I had done nothing at all that day — how could I eat his food?

"Since then, children, I have never seated myself at the table for a meal without making a private accounting as to whether I have justly and honestly earned the right to eat my daily bread..."

From the United States came a painter, who stayed in the Dvorah Barron House several months and worked indefatigably. She combed the villages and sketched dozens of figures and landscapes. This was Batya Gordon, who was born in Vilna and grew up in Chicago, but had always borne in her heart powerful longings for her native source. She would always say:

"These people look like our forefathers, like Jacob when he came from Haran. It just happened that they accidentally stayed there three thousand years..."

Batya Gordon painted the portraits of many children of all the communities. She painted the Indian girl whose gazelle's eyes shone with a calm inner light, and the hothead of the class in whose eyes the desert still flamed.

Batya, of whom we grew very fond, really thinking of her as "one of ourselves", returned to the United States, her portfolio filled with landscapes of the old-new Lachish and portraits of its first settlers, from every country and of every age. This was a warm, living greeting from Lachish to the Jews of the United States.

In the guest book of the Dvorah Barron House, the Prime Minister, who stayed there on a visit to the Lachish region, wrote the following words:

> "Even in a land of wonders — after fifty-four years of living in a land of wonders — the heart pounds at the sight of this wonder of wonders — the moulding together of the exiles, not a literary phrase but a living realization of Jewish experience: Czechoslovakian, Indian, Babylonian, Hungarian and tens of other countries; and at the wondrous sight of the blossoming of a wilderness which only six years ago I saw barren, unclaimed and uninhabited, and today I see filled with clusters of fruitful villages.
>
> "Nothing, indeed, is impossible for the people of wonders whose name is the people of Israel — and we, or those after us, will yet see the great miracle of the total redemption of both the people and the land."
>
> Signed,
D. Ben-Gurion

XXIV

WHO SHALL TEACH THE TEACHER?

AFTER A VISIT to India, Knesset Member Rachel Tsabri told me about the schools in the Indian villages. The Indian government does not build a school before it has explained the need for it to the population, nor until it has received the agreement of the public to take an active part in building the school. The village must allot land for this purpose — a serious matter in Indian villages, for the land required includes not only the lot for the school building, but also building lots for the teachers' houses and the fields allocated to each teacher. The teacher in the Indian village receives part of his salary from the inhabitants of the village, and the best means of assuring this is a plot of land. The village works the land for the benefit of the teacher, and he receives the yield of rice as payment for his work. In order to carry out all these arrangements, it is sometimes necessary to move all the houses in the village to another location . . .

At this point in the story, I interrupted the narrator.

"And what benefit does the village derive from all this?" I asked.

"First of all," she explained, "you don't see even one broken window-pane in a school or in any other public building in an Indian village. And most important: the village is proud of its school."

In comparison, here one can find village kindergartens that are closed for weeks in the winter months, because of the broken window-panes that the Council has grown tired of replacing time after time!

The state provides eight years of education, in addition to compulsory kindergarten. The children of new immigrants are supplied with books, study equipment, meals and even additional help for retarded pupils; but to this day, after twelve years of the state's existence, schools for immigrant children have not attained the same educational level existing in those attended by children of long-time residents in the country. The gap between the two types of school is still a wide one. The Minister of Education, Zalman Aranne, once summed this up sadly:

"A great love of Israel streams down from on high, but it has no echo here below..."

Once during our second year in Lachish, I went to Tel Aviv for the Sabbath, returning on the first bus that left for Beer Sheva on Sunday. The bus was packed with people, among them a large number of young women soldier-teachers returning to their duties in the villages of the Negev. There were no vacant seats, so I took my stand beside a bench where two of them were sitting. They both took out their knitting and devoted themselves to it energetically during the entire trip.

From their conversation, I gathered that they were teachers in one of the schools in the Negev with which I was well-acquainted. They were discussing the Department of Education's new regulation requiring all teachers to be at school by eight o'clock on Sunday mornings, just as on any other day of the week. The regulation was intended primarily for schools of immigrant children, whose teachers came from considerable distances, and for that reason, would often start the school day on Sunday two or three hours later than usual. The teachers in the bus with me discussed ways and means of getting around the annoying rule that forced them to rise at five in the morning after they had gone to bed in the early hours of the same morning.

"What's so terrible about it if once a week classes start at ten and finish later?" they complained. "How can you ask a teacher to get up before sunrise?"

I recalled Pinchas, the dairyman from the experimental station in Rechovot, who used to disturb our sleep when he got up to milk the cows at three in the morning. This strong young man had been used to early rising for years, especially on the Sabbath and on holidays, for labour was then one of the basic principles of our lives. Once I asked Pinchas if he didn't find it hard to get up when all the rest of the world was still sleeping. Pinchas replied that it was a matter of habit. Nevertheless, I remember one summer when early rising was very hard for him. He will not forget that summer easily — and perhaps for other reasons, as well...

At the time he was a young man working on his father's farm in Ben-Shemen. Together with his father, he milked sixteen cows three times a day, and immediately after milking, the milk was shipped to the city so that it would still be fresh on arrival. Pinchas was then spending his evenings in the company of a young girl (it may now be revealed — they have grandchildren), and he would try to persuade her to keep him company till three in the morning — he was afraid to go home before that hour, for he knew that if he laid his head on his pillow, he would instantly fall asleep, and no power on earth would be able to get him up in time for the early milking.

In the summer of that year, Pinchas got by with only his noon nap. His father could not understand what had happened to his son, for he was forced to wake Pinchas from his noon nap by dragging him out of bed by main force: otherwise he failed to wake up.

"Youngsters," Pinchas remarked. "They've got strength enough for anything."

More people got into the crowded bus at one of the stops, elderly people among them. One of the teachers who was knitting threw me a quick glance: I had been standing beside her for over half an hour, and apparently she was feeling uncomfortable about it. She made a hesitant movement — was she offering me her seat? No, I erred. The young woman sighed and went on with her knitting...

On another occasion, I joined the seventh grade on a trip

they made to Jerusalem. The teacher of the class was talented and industrious. We all respected her, and I was proud of her achievements.

We completed our tour on Mount Herzl. We took a city bus in order to return to the central bus station. The bus was completely empty. I got in first, seated all the pupils on one side of the bus, and sat down on the back bench. The young teacher got in and sat down beside with the children. I was sunk in thought, and paid little attention to what was going on.

Suddenly I recognized the voice of the young teacher, raised in argument. I roused myself and was shocked: the bus was filled with people, for it was the hour when workers were going home. The teacher was arguing with an old woman standing beside her, trying to justify her pupils, who had not offered their seats to the elderly people who stood crowded together in the bus. The teacher stated vehemently that the children had risen early and had travelled to Jerusalem from distant Lachish, and had spent most of the day on their feet. Her passionate defence touched the heart... of the pupils, who listened to her words with admiration.

There was a flaw in the planning of the regional school in Nehora, and it was our fault. In the beginning, this school was intended to serve only four villages, none of which was more than two kilometres away from the village centre, and the children could reach school on foot.

A second centre was planned for the more distant villages, but for various reasons this plan was cancelled, and our regional school in Nehora had to accept pupils from another three villages, all of which were from three to five kilometres away.

For this reason, the plan for the children to walk to school was cancelled, and arrangements had to be made for organized transportation for the children. The problem was complicated, and had to be solved immediately. We also had to find some arrangement for providing an escort for the children, as it was against the law to transport children without adult supervision. It was unfeasible to ask the parents to undertake the supervision in turn, as is customary in the older settlements: village society had not yet progressed to the point where the settlers would recognize their obligation to undertake public responsibilities of this kind.

In the development areas, the Department of Education assigned the job of supervision to the teachers themselves, but this arrangement met with outspoken opposition, and even resulted in a formal complaint to the Teachers' Union, as though this duty constituted an insufferable infringement of the basic rights of the teacher. Nevertheless, the teachers in our school finally agreed to give two hours a week to transportation supervision; and they abided by their agreement for three years running. But after this concession on their part, I did not dare approach them with any request for voluntary services required by other important school activities, such as helping in the library, supervising the pupils during recess, and so forth. Moreover, the struggle to obtain their consent to provide regular supervision for the school buses greatly damaged the educational atmosphere in the school, and did more harm than good.

Two years after the regional school was founded, we received a warning of the state of affairs developing in the school. The newspaper "Davar" published an article by a distinguished journalist who had frequently visited Nehora, staying in the home of a relative who was married to one of our permanent teachers. There was no doubt that the man had a thorough, first-hand acquaintance with the problems, and that he foresaw the outcome:

"... Only a great writer could fully describe the tragic dispute — is it indeed inevitable, and if so, even more tragic? — between the couple burning with a desire to help their newly-arrived brothers and with devotion to their ideal, and between the younger generation, the young men and women teachers in particular, who regard the aging couple as "Zionists" who have no place in a self-respecting 'society', in one that is constantly striving for increased social benefits, which it will not sacrifice on the altar of 'Zionism'."

Was the dispute indeed inevitable, and if so — even more tragic? Who can tell? In any case, it occurred. Were it not for the friendly personal help of the supervisor A. Shakhrai, who did not stint his labours in removing the obstacles from my path, I would have been forced to leave the school long before I did.

I saw many instances of humane endeavour among the young women teachers, some of which required constant effort. In one of the villages lived a young girl who contracted infantile paralysis and was left a cripple. The Department of Education sent a teacher to her home to give her a private lesson an hour a day, but the child's mother pleaded with me to accept her into the school, so that she would not grow up isolated from the society of other children. I left the decision on this request up to the teacher herself. She agreed, and accordingly took it upon herself — as did the teachers who later replaced her, and the drivers — to carry the child to and from the school bus and up the steps every day. The pupils also learned from their example and behaved in the same way, and the crippled girl became an important educational factor in the life of our school.

The Israeli youth who complete the teachers' seminars seem to be very talented in handicrafts. I was always amazed at the inventiveness of the teachers in decorating their classrooms, in arranging performances and celebrations, in giving form to the most elementary subjects. As for themselves personally, the young women gave the institution an aesthetic variety — the magic of their youth! Once at a Purim party, at the end of a successful celebration, the teachers prepared a surprise for their pupils: they themselves dressed up as school children. When they came onto the stage in short dresses, with school satchels on their backs and ribbons in their hair, they gave a performance — under the direction of another teacher — of a disorderly class. They showed their pupils, as though in a distorting mirror, all the problems and frictions of an ordinary school day — a disorderly roll call, forgetting notebooks, talking during class, grabbing food from the table, singing false notes in choir practice. The children paid delighted attention, and learned another lesson through their gales of laughter.

On another occasion I was present, together with Mordecai and an experienced teacher who was our guest, at a teachers' party at the end of the school year. After giving out the yearly certificates, the teachers went into the dining-hall and sat down around the table. The young people were in a good mood, and in no hurry to break up. They themselves were unable to evaluate the importance of the work they had done during the year. But they sensed that they had passed through a valuable experience, an unforgettable period in their lives.

The young men and women at the party sang and made a good deal of noise. From the kitchen they brought huge pots and frying pans and platters. To the sound of a deafening "orchestra", people began to arrive and gather — the watchmen first, and afterwards the other residents of Nehora, who had been awakened from their sleep and had come to see what was going on. In the end, they were all drawn into the circle of dancers.

The three older people who chanced to be there held their breath and were glad that their presence did not distract the gay band, nor stifle the overflowing joy of youth. The older people knew that in hours like these, young people store up strength for the future — for days of weariness and trial, and for days in which they have no pleasure...

I read Makarenko's *Pedagogic Poem* many times. I sought to learn from it everything that might be of use in the solution of our problems in this period of the Ingathering of the Exiles. I had read and heard much about the activities of teachers in

America fifty years ago, during their period of "Ingathering". I had many discussions with a teacher of long experience, a guest from the United States, who was a supervisor of schools in one of the boroughs of New York where many immigrant families from Puerto Rico had settled. The schools of that borough were flooded with children who did not speak English at home, and whose standard of living was extremely low. In most of these immigrant families, the mother was also forced to work, to help support the family, and the children were neglected and wandered around the streets.

During that period, many of the borough's old residents removed their children from the public schools and transferred them to private schools, where, of course, there were no "street children". The municipal authorities of New York interfered. Investigations were made, and the authorities took various steps to prevent racial discrimination taking root among the population.

I asked the American teacher: "What did you actually do?"

"We sought the common denominator," she replied. "The educational goal that united everyone, such as love of one's country. We encouraged the feeling of patriotism. Every morning a flag-raising ceremony was held in every school. We assigned many classroom duties and distributed many marks for outstanding progress. We sought symbols that would attract the child, and make his period of adjustment easier."

Makarenko did exactly the same thing under a form of government totally different from that of the United States.

We chose a beautiful name for our school — the name of the late poet, David Shimoni, the poet of the land of Eretz-Israel, and of his own specific "Torah of Eretz-Israel". On the flag we embroidered the legend: "The David Shimoni Public Regional School". We sewed a case for the flag and kept it in a place of honour when it was not in use. We elected pupils to act as flag-bearers, both for the national flag and for the school flag. In the centre of the field where we held roll-call we erected a flagpole where the flag was raised on holidays and special occasions. The children learned how to blow bugles, to raise the flag and to lower it to half-mast when necessary. Jewish children outside the country had never dreamed of anything like this.

We achieved all this over a considerable period, and if we overdid it to some degree — it was done in order to present ideas which were opposed to the general mood of the country, the mood of disparagement of the Keren Hakayemet and of "Zionism".

On the Tenth Anniversary Year of the State of Israel, the Keren Hakayemet decided to divide the country into eighteen areas, and to present each area with a special flag.

The David Shimoni School in Nehora received the flag of the Lachish area to keep during the Tenth Anniversary Year.

A selected group of the best pupils in school went to Jerusalem a day before vacation, on the eve of Rosh Hashana. Our group left with a young teacher and myself. In the city, we formed a double line with our school flag at the head. Together with pupils from the other areas, we marched to the President's home, where we received the regional flag and the President's blessing. From there we went to the National Buildings, where we attended the traditional presentation ceremony of the Jerusalem standard to the outstanding school in the country. In short, we had a marvellous day.

When we boarded the bus on our way home, I put the two flags (the school flag and the new Keren Hakayemet flag that we had just received) into their cases and put them on the luggage rack above the seat. I put the two flagpoles on the floor, and made the flag-bearers responsible for them. Then I myself sat down, and dozed until we reached Masmiya.

When we got out of the bus, it was already dark. The truck of the Lachish Area Council was there, waiting to take us home. The teacher counted the pupils — they were all there.

"Are the flags here?" I asked.

"Yes, they're here."

The truck started out. Then one of the pupils spoke up.

"Teacher, the flags aren't here!"

The pupil who had said he had them was holding only the flag-poles. The flags themselves remained in their case on the luggage rack in the bus.

I said to the teacher, "Take the boy who's responsible for the flags with you, and try to get a lift to Rechovot. Maybe you can catch the bus there."

The teacher was taken aback. "Where would I go to look for them? Let's wait till morning, and decide what to do then."

There was no time to lose. I said, "Then take the children home. I'll try to get to Rechovot myself."

I ran to the deserted highway. In those days, few people travelled the roads of the south after dark: the Sinai Campaign and the prolonged operations of infiltrators were still too close. A taxi passed without stopping. I thought to myself: "Tomorrow is the eve of Rosh Hashana. All the public transportation is crowded today. Who knows where the bus will be in the morning?"

I saw a truck approaching, and determined to make it stop no matter what. I actually flew into the middle of the road. The driver slammed on his brakes and jumped down from his seat.

"Are you out of your mind?" he shouted. "Do you want to commit suicide?"

I didn't know what to say. I said, "Please do me a favour and take me to Rechovot right away. I've lost something very valuable on the bus."

"I guarantee that you won't find it..."

"I must get there! I'll pay whatever you want to charge me."

The driver helped me climb up onto the high seat and increased his speed. On the way, I told him that I had lost two flags. His reaction was surprising: he literally rolled with laughter.

"What a character! Standing at the crossroads in the middle of the night looking for flags! And I was thinking, who knows what treasure she's lost!"

I managed to reach the bus before it left the Rechovot station. I took the cases from the luggage rack and went to spend the night in the home of friends in Rechovot.

When I returned in the morning and came into the schoolyard, the hive was humming in its usual fashion. One of the teachers was holding a rehearsal with the children on the large porch, for the ceremony of the reception of the Lachish flag, which was to take place in another three hours — representatives of all the schools in the area were to take part in it. I thought: Here they are, preparing to raise the canopy without knowing whether the bridegroom will reach it or not. Apparently the concept of "a flag" had not taken root in our consciousness — not like the Book of Torah.

At eleven o'clock the guests arrived, and the flags were out. The ceremony was impressive, but I felt somehow unsatisfied. I thought to myself: What can be done so that the children won't grow up thinking the way that truck-driver thought, who sympathized only with 'valuable' losses?

I gained a feeling of satisfaction only several months later, quite unexpectedly. When only the two of us were in the teachers' room, the same young teacher who had been with me that night addressed me.

"If you only knew," she said. "how much that business with the flag hurt me, and how sorry I was about it!"

From that moment, in my eyes, the young woman grew up and became a teacher.

XXV

EAST AND WEST

If I were asked what we have learned during these years among new people in a new land, my reply would be: we have learned to respect tolerance. The new settlers, too, have learned this to a great degree. This does not mean that their basic viewpoint has changed: a change of values is a slow process.

During our first days in Noga, we were awakened in the middle of the night by unusual shouts. Cautiously, we left the hut and crawled to the centre of the village. The light of the full moon revealed a very odd scene, The young woman instructor, who had gone out for the evening to another village, had returned at a late hour accompanied by a friend, a young man. When the couple entered the village, the watchmen surrounded them, and at the shouts of the watchmen, the settlers had awakened and come out of their houses. Now they were all heaping abuse on her, accusing her of being a loose woman, and the young woman was crying helplessly.

Incidents like these are already a thing of the past, but this does not mean that the residents of the new villages have changed their views about relations between the sexes.

When Lake Zohar was being constructed, a restaurant was set up in Nehora for the workers. The restaurant employed girls from the nearby villages who worked in two shifts. The restaurant owner's car made several trips a day to the nearby city in order to bring the necessary supplies. All of us were accustomed to getting a lift with this car.

One of the village girls finished her work late at night, and the driver took her home. In the early hours of the morning, the ambulance was summoned to take the girl to the hospital.

Her parents' suspicions of her behaviour had hurt her deeply, and she had tried to commit suicide.

After completing her studies, our daughter went to basic training camp and a month later, in August, she came to visit us on furlough, a soldier in uniform. Like all privates, she was proud of her new uniform, but the settlers in the villages were shocked by it.

At the beginning of the school year, one of the best girl pupils of eighth grade, for whom we had great hopes, did not appear in school. After several days we began to ask questions, and to investigate the matter: was anyone sick at home? Had she been sent to work in the field? We learned from the other pupils that she was at home. We asked the woman instructor in her village to find out the reason for her absence. The instructor came back and told us that it wasn't a simple affair: the girl's parents were tight-mouthed and refused to answer any questions on the subject. We began to suspect that her parents were plotting to arrange their daughter's marriage before she was of legal age.

When our daughter came to visit us on a Sabbath, she was shocked when she heard that the girl, of whom she was also very fond, had left school. As she was on good terms with the girl's family, she walked over to the village to see what had happened. She returned quickly embarrassed and offended: they had not welcomed her as they had formerly, and they had refused to speak to her...

I decided to go to see them myself and clear the matter up. I went to the house of my pupil in the other village, and spoke to her sternly:

"You cannot leave school in such a fashion — without saying goodbye to the class or to the teachers, without thanking them, and without returning your books to the school! Tomorrow at eight you must report at the school. Otherwise, I shall be forced, to my regret, to call the police."

On my way home, I came to the conclusion that I had

taken a risky step: if the girl did not come to school, I would be a laughing-stock. And of what use would the police be in a case like this?

The girl did not appear the next day. Instead, her mother appeared, accompanied by a young man who spoke Hebrew and served as an interpreter. The mother attacked the problem at once, and spoke plainly.

"They gossip about you anyhow, that you teach girls to go into the army — and here, your *daughter!*"

And she gave me a piercing look. Could I look her in the eye?

I understood: during the course of time, the settlers in the villages had gotten used to women soldier-teachers and other kinds of women soldiers who served the villages in various capacities; but to them, this was a foreign custom which did not apply to them. Having no alternative, uneducated and helpless people were forced to accept the services of anyone who offered them without examining their morals too closely. Thus they had accepted the necessary services "there", even from *goyim*. But there is a limit to everything, and it was unthinkable that the "anathema" of girls being conscripted into the army should affect them as well...

When I immigrated to Eretz-Israel from Russia, I had behind me several years of life under the Soviet government, which had immediately declared the full liberation of women from the tyrannical control of men. My young head was full of enthusiastic slogans in support of our righteous struggle for equal rights. But when I encountered the Arab women of this country for the first time, the wives of *fellahin* and of *effendis,* I decided that my own husband was an utterly righteous man.

In those first days in the country, I was once making my way through the deep sand dunes of the old Rechovot at noon on a scorching summer day. In front of me an Arab was riding on a donkey, shading himself from the rays of the sun with a black parasol. Behind him walked a barefoot woman with an infant in her arms. I would not have guessed that one had any connection at all with the other, had the Arab not halted his donkey and kicked off the shoes that were chafing him. Without saying a word, the woman picked up the shoes, and continued to stride through the sand behind her husband...

On another occasion an Arab peddler selling oranges passed by our house in the morning, crying his wares in a loud voice:

"*Marantsim! Marantsim!*"

Our neighbour, whose wife was a nurse who had been working on night shift and was now sleeping, tried to hush the Arab.

"Shh ... Shh!" he said. "My wife is sleeping ..."

The Arab felt sorry for the stupid Jew and gave him a piece of advice: "Why should she be sleeping, when you get up? Give her a kick, and she'll get up!"

When she accepted the sentence: "*He who teaches his daughter Torah, it is as though he teaches her folly*", the Jewish woman of the Eastern communities took upon herself the yoke of submission and self-effacement. In the few places where absolute patriarchal rule still exists, the life of a young woman is hard and bitter. To this day it is almost impossible for the old people among the new immigrants from Eastern countries to grasp the difference between the legal and moral approach to family affairs that existed in the country of their origin, and that which exists in the "Land of the Patriarchs." The instances in which the government is on the woman's side are incomprehensible to the men.

A beautiful young woman of twenty worked in our school restaurant. She had been married to a man in Morocco when she was very young, and had already become the mother of a daughter at the age of seventeen. When the family came to Israel, her husband was discovered to be suffering from tuberculosis. He was immediately taken to the hospital and did not leave his sickbed till the day of his death, some two years later.

The young widow and her little daughter lived in the home of her husband's parents. Unluckily, her husband had been an only son. The parents, who had paid good money for her to a poor family, regarded her as their private property. As is the custom among the Eastern immigrants, the family settled in the same village with its many relatives, and together they

formed a strong 'khamula', or clan; while the young woman had neither relative nor friend in the country. Her parents and brothers who had remained in Morocco had relinquished their rights to her, so to speak, and she was at the mercy of her parents-in-law.

The deep sorrow of the parents during the lengthy mortal illness of their only son was worsened by the fact that their young daughter-in-law was beautiful and blooming, as though the tragedy had not affected her at all. She worked in the school kitchen and was well-liked by all of us. The only people who constantly complained of her were her husband's aged parents. Their main complaint was that "she doesn't cry a lot." The parents and their relatives spied on her and nagged her whenever they had the least shadow of a suspicion that her behaviour might possibly not have been exactly what they thought it should be.

When news of the son's death arrived from the hospital,

the bereaved father burst into the school kitchen with a knife in his hand and accused his daughter-in-law of being the cause of her husband's death. According to him, his son had died of love for his wife, who had never loved him. We barely managed to save the young widow from the hands of the frenzied old man, who was almost out of his mind with grief.

We kept her hidden in the house of one of the teachers for several days. She did not walk behind her husband's coffin, for the entire village was up in arms against her. They all identified themselves with the bereaved parents, and censured the daughter-in-law for not having loved her husband and for not being sad enough during his illness, even though his parents had paid good money for her.

We went to the parents' home to ask for the personal belongings of their daughter-in-law, who had with her only the dress she was wearing. A memorial candle made of a wick dipped in oil burned for thirty days in the home of the griefstricken parents, darkening with smoke walls that were already dark. The little girl, who was dressed in a long, ill-fitting gown, clung to her grandmother, who showered her with kisses and words of affection in Arabic.

We quickly discovered that we had no common language with these old people, although we had brought interpreters with us, and the old man himself understood Hebrew.

"How should she have any clothes?" he said. "We paid for her in Morocco, and we bought her all her clothes. Her family is poor, completely worthless!"

"But we all know that she's been working hard for two years. She earned her bread, and brought you the money. Couldn't she have bought herself clothes with the money she gave you?"

"How could she have any money of her own?" the old man argued aggressively. "She's a married woman, she's not permitted to keep money. We'll sell her belongings to put up a monument on our son's grave..."

"But if she decides to take the little girl away from you, and to cease all relations with you — why, you'll be all alone! You'd better think it over. The little girl is now fatherless, and she belongs to her mother, according to the laws of the country."

We were very hesitant about using this argument, for a man should not be judged in the hour of his grief, and we felt sorry for the bereaved parents. But the old man burst out laughing — we seemed completely ludicrous in his eyes.

"How could she 'take the little girl away'? Why, *we* raised her from the day she was born, and she's *ours*. What do you mean, 'she's fatherless'? *I'm* still alive! I'd like to see a government that could take her away from me!..."

In another instance, one of our school cooks got married, a girl who had worked in the school kitchen for three years and had become very friendly with all the teachers. She went to evening classes and courses in handicrafts. This young woman already had a strong desire for a "new life". When she married, she brought a "dowry" with her, which is not customary among Eastern Jews. She had saved part of her salary every month, putting it in the bank, and after the wedding she furnished her new home with modern equipment and other treasured possessions. She bought a gas stove, the pioneer of "gas" in the village; a red china figurine of a horse with a gilded saddle stood on the radio. Behind the glass panes of the buffet stood a variety of dishes, little used, but to be found in the homes of every young married couple in the villages. These dishes add importance to the new nest, and are a testimony to the number of friends who brought wedding gifts. The young cook continued to work in the school after her marriage, for there were many other things she wanted to buy with her salary. She continued working until one day, when she simply did not appear. Afterwards we were told that she had left her home without a quarrel, and had gone away, no one knew where: there was a misunderstanding between her and her husband.

There was a stormy debate among the workers in the school on the subject of the Eastern woman in revolt. Everyone discerned signs of a change in values in this affair, and the beginning of the liberation of the woman from her enslavement to her husband.

But the parents of the young woman were in a state of shock. Their daughter had left the village and the house of her parents, and how could they look people in the face any longer? The woman instructor went to the deserted husband to try to discover what had happened. He told a simple story: she hadn't prepared a lunch for him to take with him when he went to work in the morning, and when he reminded her of this in the evening, she replied that she had to go to work too, just the same as he did...

I asked the instructor to explain to him that he was in the wrong. His wife also worked outside the home, work that was difficult and responsible, and in addition to this, she did all the housekeeping. Instead of complaining about her, wouldn't it be better if he helped her a little?...

Here the mother-in-law, who was well-known in the village as a "woman of valour" interrupted.

"That's the whole trouble," she said. "The whole time she's looking at how the *Ashkenazim* live! She's forgotten the old ways, and she hasn't learned the new ones yet. She has to learn that the husband is the *head* and that the house must be in order, and that's the main thing. What's this 'fair' and 'unfair'? He doesn't have to be fair! What did he do to her? Did he beat her? Did he drive her out of the house? He only said "The food's no good." So tell him, "I'm sorry, tomorrow I'll make a good meal for you." If she doesn't obey her husband, they'll raise bad children who don't respect their father. Why marry at all, in that case?..."

I fear I must admit that there is a certain amount of truth

in the words of the old woman, who has raised half a dozen sons who obey her and show her the greatest respect.

One of the young men in the village fell in love with a nice young girl, but her parents did not approve of the match, and put every obstacle possible in the young man's way. When the young man sent representatives to ask for the girl's hand, her father claimed that people had seen the young man, smoking on the Sabbath... The young man took an oath that he would smoke no more, even on weekdays. But the girl's father hardened his heart and made the conditions for his consent more difficult, and the negotiations went on for a considerable time. There must be a certain sum of money, a certain amount of jewellery, and so on. Every ornament he bought her, its price and form, the dresses and the furniture — each of these served as the subject of prolonged bargaining which did not always end peacably. Meanwhile the poor young man grew thin and pale — he had barely exchanged a word with his beloved, as she was always under the strictest chaperonage of parents and brothers. The bridegroom worked from morning till night to raise the huge sum the bride's parents demanded of him.

The requirements for a proper wedding include a sea of *arak,* the famous flautist from the village of Patish, and a dancer from a nightclub in Jaffa. When the great day arrived, the yard was lit with two strings of electric lights, all the benches from the school and the clubhouse were brought to the yard, and even the little chairs from the kindergarten were loaned for the event. Not a man from the village was absent at this magnificent wedding, and even infants were taken from their cradles to take part in the rejoicing...

The bridegroom's friends served the guests with refreshments, a service that is regarded as a signal honour for those who perform it. All the children of the village sat on the ground quietly and politely, enchanted by the electric light and the marvellous flute of the famous Aziz from Patish. The fat songstress-dancer performed enthusiastically. She sang in a hoarse voice, moved her hips, and gave fervent cries in Arabic. Then she came down from the stage into the crowd of guests and clashed small cymbals which were attached to her fingers actually in the ears of the guests. She showed special attention to those who appeared to be the village dignitaries. Her chosen "victim" would fling coins into her low-cut dress. God only knows how this custom coexists together with the standards of indubitable modesty of the Kurdish girls in the village, all of whom were present! In any case, the successful dancer's bosom swelled with coins...

The couple began to build up their farm in the village. The young woman was strong and healthy, but her husband grew thin and gaunt. Indeed, there were many absolute necessities for the household, unknown to an earlier generation: various furnishings, electrical appliances, a combination radiogram almost as large as a desk, which miraculously changed by itself the records of "Ichikadana" and "Rumia"! The area in vegetables that had to be cultivated was too large. The young husband could barely manage his work on the farm, and the poor young man was hiring himself out as a watchman at night...

"What's the matter with you?" I asked him. "Here, you've realized your dream, and you've got your beloved — you ought to be growing fat with contentment!"

The young man admitted to me that the work on the farm was hard and heavy, and there was so much to do, and he had no help...

"Doesn't your wife help you with any of it?"

"No, she only takes care of the house. She says that the nurse doesn't allow pregnant women to work in the field. When I ask her 'Come to the field with me for just a little while,' right away she says, 'Come with me to the nurse,' and I'm embarrassed..."

Apparently the child-care nurse, who also cared for the

pregnant women in the village, had filled his measure to overflowing with her devoted attention to the young bride...

We have already had the privilege of seeing girl pupils from the villages in Lachish who did not quit school at the earliest permissible age, but continued their education and entered high school. In the ninth and tenth grades in Nehora, there are girls who are just as able as the boys are in their studies, and who even outshine them when it comes to performances and public appearances. And thus a new generation of young women from the Eastern communities is growing up.

We took one of the classes for a hike in the fields to gather heads of grain for the "seven varieties" of the Festival of First Fruits. A combine was working in the field, and we went over to look at this versatile machine that mows, threshes, bales the straw and pours the grain into a truck as though by magic. The one young man working on the combine did not appear to be especially busy: he joked with pupils and teachers while the machine laboured on like a magic robot with the strength of dozens of horses.

Following the combine was an aged woman, bent over and walking slowly. She was the grandmother of one of the pupils, out gathering the gleanings of the field, just as the women did in the days of Ruth the Moabite. At home she would wash them, dry them in the sun, and for weeks afterwards sit on the ground and grind them by hand between two round grinding-stones — as if nothing on earth had changed during thousands of years...

XXVI

"WHERE THE OUTPOST USED TO BE..."

A LINE FROM a nostalgic popular Israeli ballad says: "Where the outpost used to be, there sits a town." It has real meaning here — Kiryat-Gat was built on the site of the outpost of "Iraq-el-Manshiyeh". In the days of the War of Independence, there was a common grave, for eighty-seven of our soldiers who fell here. When the grave was transferred to Army Cemeteries, a memorial column was erected and a grove planted on the spot.

Kiryat-Gat can be seen from afar, and rows of three-storied apartment buildings have sprung up along the main highway. When you compare the way it looked five years ago with the way it looks today, you might well think that an entire city had fallen out of the heavens.

Yet the birth pangs of the capital of the Lachish region were hard. Its growth is a problem even today. Its founder and first administrator was the late Yitzchak Tchijek, member of a family that has played a great part in building and defending the country. He accomplished much, but his days were few. After him, the administrative head of the entire region, Levi Argov, guided the progress of the city that was being built until Gideon Naor was appointed — a young mayor, according to Lachish's tradition of youth.

As late as 1956 we read in one of the newspapers: "A city? Has Kiryat-Gat the right to be called a city? It exists as a city only because of the determination of a few obstinate men who decided to build a group of buildings in the heart of the desert.."

At first, most of the settlers in Lachish nicknamed it *"ma'abarat* Kiryat-Gat", or even *"moshav* Kiryat-Gat". The appearance of the city was that of a typical *ma'abara*. The first of its residents, from Morocco, lived in tin huts, for no other housing existed.

Kiryat-Gat is an artificial city — the realization of a daring idea: to build a capital for the reviving region of Lachish. The location of the new city was planned on a site almost equidistant (about 50 kilometres) from Jerusalem, Beer Sheva, and Tel Aviv. In the beginning, in memory of the Philistine city of Gat, the new city was named "Gata". However people, began to pronounce it "Getteh", "Gita", and even "Gittl", and the authorities quickly renamed it with its present name. On a broadcast over Kol Israel in February 1957, we heard an interviewer speaking with people over the telephone. He asked various people in Tel Aviv where Kiryat Gat was. No one had heard of it, and no one knew where it was located in the Lachish region.

The plan of Kiryat Gat was born in 1955, when representatives of the Zionist Federation in Britain visited Jerusalem and took part in the foundation of "The Anglo-Israeli Corporation for the Development of Kiryat Gat". This corporation had as a goal the encouragement of concentrated settlement in Kiryat-Gat of youth from England. For this purpose a neighbourhood of improved apartments was built which to this day bears the name of "the Anglo-saxon quarter", although few "Anglo-saxons" live in it.

At the end of the Sinai Campaign, the stream of immigrants from North Africa increased, and, surprisingly, that gate which had been closed for tens of years was opened: a wave of immigration arrived from the countries of the "people's democracies".

Two years later, when the representatives of the Federation from England revisited the spot, they were astonished at the sight of the city, which already had a population of 4,000 (of whom only 40 families were from England.) This was more than had been estimated. According to the first plan, the city's population was to have reached 6,000 over a period of five years. It was necessary to alter the plan of the city and enlarge it enormously.

"WHERE THE OUTPOST USED TO BE..."

The first builders of Kiryat Gat planned to give the new development town an agricultural character, and subsidiary farms of 1.5 dunams were distributed to its first settlers. Today, planners think that during the next five years Kiryat Gat will grow to a population of 25,000.

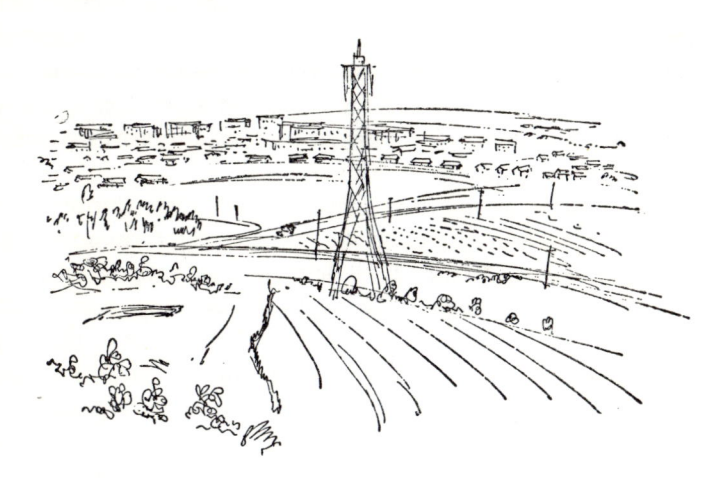

Industrial circles took the initiative and erected in Kiryat Gat a new industrial centre outside the dangerous strip of Tel Aviv–Haifa. Nevertheless, it was hard to balance and direct the growth of the city which burst out and spread uncontrollably. It was also hard to satisfy an unemployed man with promises of what the future would bring. The young city has passed through frequent crises. Well-remembered are the riots in the Labour Exchange, accompanied by broken furniture, and the strike which broke out in Kiryat Gat during the days of the strike in Noga. The harassing question of "how shall we earn our living" still worries many families of elderly and physically incapacitated people, who appear with every wave of mass immigration.

North African immigrants comprise most of the population

of Kiryat Gat, and they play a great part in every field of its life. But Kiryat Gat also had the honour of absorbing thousands of the first immigrants from Eastern Europe. Till that time, the Lachish region was populated almost wholly by immigrants from Asia and North Africa.

"*And our eyes shall see thy return to Zion with mercy.*" The immigration which reached us from behind the iron curtain came to Israel by the grace of God. The situation of the Jews there is well known. Here is an excerpt from a letter of Lyova Eliav, the former regional head of Lachish, afterwards secretary of the Israel Embassy in Moscow.

"... I brought my two children with their Purim noise-makers to the synagogue on the evening of the reading of the scroll of Esther. Hundreds of Jews listened tensely to Zvika and Ofra rattling their noisemakers for all they were worth. These Jews heard in this unmusical noise the notes of the harps we hanged up on the willows beside the rivers of Babylon, when we left Zion. In the end, the noise-makers passed into the hands of Jewish children who keep them as their dearest possessions. Let us hope that the day will come when these noise-makers will sound on the plains of Lachish, when their present owners will come — and they must come — to us..."

Nevertheless, when they came to us, we encountered problems of a completely new kind.

I met one of the immigrants from Russia on the bus, on my way to Tel Aviv. She was an elderly woman, and with her was a young man of about twenty. I offered her the empty seat beside me. The young man sat in front of us. The woman answered my questions in Yiddish, and told me that she and her son had arrived from Warsaw a month ago. They had no relatives at all in the country. The son had not found suitable work, and they were seeking a way to return...

I asked her what made her wish to return to her "native" land, and her words burst forth like steam. Her sharp tongue did not spare anything — the State of Israel, its government, its laws, and its citizens — they were all ill-intentioned rascals. Her only son was a photographer, and he needed work in his profession. Here they explain to him that he ought to change his profession, as there is little work for photographers in the country. But under no circumstances will she agree that her son take a hoe or a hammer in his hand for even one day. They suffered enough under Hitler — her husband was killed, and the entire family was destroyed. And they are entitled to a place to live and a respectable livelihood! And if not — then who needs this state? Workers in America take the bread out of their mouths to donate money for helping new immigrants here. And here they told *her* to take a broom and sweep the streets of the city for wages of four pounds a day!...

I replied cautiously.

"And what's so terrible about it? We've heard that even in the United States, the "greenhorn", who doesn't know the language of the country, is willing to take whatever work he can get in order to earn a living. And what's the matter with a broom, if the work isn't too hard for you?"

My words produced a wave of reproaches and criticism. Other people in the bus began to join in the argument. The son, who seemed to be indifferent to the entire matter, turned his head and plucked at his mother's sleeve.

I noticed the vast difference in the reactions of the mother and of her son. I asked her if her son spoke Yiddish. No, he didn't speak a word. And Russian? No, he only understood Polish. I was sorry that I didn't speak Polish, I though that it would be better if I could speak to the young man himself. Perhaps he would be more flexible than his mother, and it would be easier to convince him that it was worth his while to think about changing his occupation while he was still young.

I asked the mother, quite innocently: "What's your name?"

The son looked at me, and opened his mouth for the first

time. He answered with a question in Russian: "What do you want to know our name for?"

His mother tried to calm him, and answered in Russian: "Don't worry, Yeffim, the lady doesn't mean any harm..."

I invited the mother and her son to visit us in Nehora. I told her that there was a chance of getting both work and housing in our village centre. In order to make the visit easier for them, I suggested a convenient plan: I had friends who lived on Rothschild Boulevard, in the centre of Tel-Aviv. In the afternoon I was planning to return to Nehora with them, in their car. If the mother and son would go with me to their house, it would be easy for them to find my friends' apartment later on. In the late afternoon, we would all travel back to Nehora together, and meanwhile they would save the busfare. The distance between Kiryat-Gat and Nehora is not great, and if they did not wish to spend the night at our house, we would take them back to Kiryat-Gat.

They seemed to find the invitation attractive, for in Tel Aviv they got onto the city bus with me. But suddenly I sensed a change in them. They were overcome by a nervousness they could not disguise. They wanted to get off the bus at the first stop, claiming that they would be late at the offices of the Jewish Agency. I promised to send them to the Agency offices in a taxi from the house of my friends. This offer increased their alarm. The son whispered something to his mother, and she spoke to me in Yiddish.

"My son is already upset. Is it much farther?"

At that moment, the bus turned off Allenby and into Rothschild Boulevard. The son looked ahead with dull eyes and said in Russian, in a voice filled with despair: "We're already outside the city..."

It was already clear to me that in their eyes I was a suspicious character, and they were seeking a way to escape. We got out of the bus, and I let them walk ahead of me until we reached my friends' apartment. I introduced my friends to the mother and her son and told them that they came from Poland, and that I wanted to invite the young man to Nehora and help him find work, but he only spoke Polish, and he didn't understand me...

My friends addressed them in Polish, and here something new became apparent: neither of them understood a word of Polish! It was obvious that the young man had grown up and been educated in the Soviet Union, but for some reason he was afraid to admit the fact. Now I understood the meaning of the strange behaviour of these citizens of the land of freedom...

The young man remained silent, but the mother was not at all embarrassed when I discerned her falsehood. She kept up a stream of conversation, and promised that they would come in the afternoon and go to Nehora with us. By now she was ready to promise anything, and to do whatever was asked of her — if only she could get out of here, and get her son out of this "dangerous trap".

They parted from us, and I have not seen them since...

This incident saddened me, and more than once I asked myself: did they stay in the country? Would he succeed in becoming part of the life of the country, of this whirlpool of tribes and communities, this Yeffim who grew up among *goyim,* alone and unwanted? For I had a strong, honest desire to help him and his mother, who was almost out of her mind with love and constant fear for her only son, the sole survivor of her family...

We frequently encountered people from this new immigration that was so close to us from the standpoint of origin and language. From them we learned what Eretz-Israel had given to immigrants from the very same countries who had come directly from the death camps to Israel, and had not postponed their immigration to remain on the blood-soaked soil of a foreign country for another ten years. The people of Kfar-Achim were already different people, utterly different from these brothers of theirs who had just arrived.

On one of our visits to the "railroad quarter" — so called because the one-storied houses were built in a long, attached row — in Kiryat-Gat, where the immigrants from Poland were housed, we gave out balloons to the children who had gathered around.

A stocky, white-haired woman approached me. I drew back from her: she was waving her arms at me, and her two hands had been amputated.

"Please give me balloons for my grandchildren. They didn't get any..."

I was sorry not to be able to grant her request — the balloons had all been handed out.

I asked her how she had lost her hands. She told me one of the stories so usual among people of this immigration. There was no doubt as to its truth: her amputated hands were testimony to it. She told me that she had been sent to chop wood in Teige. The wagon which had brought her to work left without her, and she was left alone to spend the night in the Siberian forest. On that night her hands froze.

The woman invited me to her daughter's house, where she was living. In the house, her two grandchildren were sitting on the bed and blowing up the balloons they had received from me, contrary to their grandmother's claim.

I met the disabled woman a number of times, and each time I heard her complain about the country: "There it was good," she claimed.

In this immigration were many children who had not been circumcised. There were instances where pupils from this immigration scorned Bible studies, remarking that it was a religious book that was already old-fashioned: they were repeating things they had heard in former schools.

There were other instances as well, where the parents were faithful to the Jewish traditions and had immigrated in order to save their sons from defilement. They now asked the help of the teachers in bringing the hearts of their sons back to the faith of their fathers.

Among the immigrants from Eastern Europe, there were many mixed marriages: Jews married Polish women who had saved them during the war. And there were cases where a Jewish woman had married a gentile and had brought him to Eretz-Israel. I encountered a case of this kind. A couple had a lovely daughter of seventeen, who had almost completed her studies in high school in Poland. The parents told me that the only thing that had brought them to Israel was the treatment of her daughter by the community. Her schoolmates persecuted her as a Jew. Every day she would come home with tears in her eyes and tell them that they were throwing stones at her...

Blood mounted to her father's face when he told me this, and his fists clenched. "I always used to tell her: 'Hit them back, throw stones at them! Why do you say nothing to them, and come home to cry?'"

I thought to myself: A stranger wouldn't understand...

Twice a week the mayor had regular office hours for receiving the public in the municipal centre of Kiryat-Gat. By spending some time in his office during one of these periods, one can learn a great deal about the problems of a growing city.

Here one can get a clear picture of the mutual suspicion existing between immigrants from Europe and immigrants from the Eastern countries. An immigrant from Rumania wants to open a fish shop in the new shopping centre. The mayor explains to him that there are already six shops of this kind in the centre, and the man complains:

"If I were only a Moroccan..."

While the Moroccan, who enters the room next in turn, will burst out, if his request is not granted:

"We're the 'blacks', everything's for the Rumanians!..."

A family of Polish immigrants comes in: a man, a woman, and a little girl of three, and they find it hard to ask for help. The father says that whatever he does, he does well. In the "lands of freedom", he learned the law: anyone who doesn't work, doesn't eat. But he fell ill unexpectedly, and it was discovered that he had a chronic infection of the spinal cord. He was released from the hospital completely incapacitated for any physical work. His wife began working as a cleaning woman in the offices of the police station, but there were women with greater seniority rights even for this miserable work.

The man tried to control his feelings, and tell of their situation calmly, but he was unable to do so. Suddenly he dropped his face in his hands and began to sob. His wife turned her face to the wall and her shoulders shook, and the little girl, seeing her parents like this, was alarmed and burst into heart-rending cries, clinging to her mother: "Mother, come away! Let's go away from here!"

I saw the helpless young mayor in his hour of weakness...

Election days in Israel are worse than a plague. They are ten times worse in the development areas. This is the price of a democratic government, and we must accept this torment willingly. For months on end the numerous rival parties sharpen their swords, and the rivals do not hesitate to draw from their quivers the "pure" weapon of inter-community hatred. Everything that has been thrust into the dim corners of the unconscious now erupts as forcefully as though it came from an exploding pressure cooker...

I was invited to Kiryat-Gat in the afternoon for the ceremony of opening the new municipal library named after the late Rivka Alper. After the opening, when darkness fell, there was to be another ceremony for the lighting of the city streets with electricity. I saw that the municipal workers were agitated and whispering among themselves.

I heard one of them whisper to his companions: "We can't let Gideon appear before them in the dark. All the "knives' will be there. Lots of them are drunk, and they're all mad..."

When I tried to find out why Gideon should be careful about

appearing in his own city to light the streets, they told me that embittered residents were seeking an opportunity to make trouble. There were many unemployed, and also plenty of "special problems".

I asked Gideon's permission to accompany him to the ceremony of lighting the streets, and he agreed, The driver circled the city in order to get to the place where the lights were to be turned on from a direction other than that by which he was expected to arrive. On the way I talked to Gideon about the problems of the different groups of immigrants, and about the desire of immigrants from undeveloped countries to "take matters into their own hands" — a desire not in keeping with their abilities — and about the difficulty in finding a flexible mode of approach which would suit the special character of each of the tribes of Israel and would also answer the objective needs of the country as a whole.

In the darkness, the driver took us through the crowd and stopped the car directly beside the small stage that was lit with the weak light of a kerosene lamp. Gideon helped me climb up the steps. Only the two of us stood on the stage.

"What's that? A 'mama'? Is she his mama?" voices came from the crowd.

Gideon addressed the crowd:

"I would like to present a friend of our city!"

The mayor's words struck me like a blow: I had not expected this at all! I had had no intention of speaking here! I had not been asked to speak in advance, and I had no speech prepared...

However, I understood one thing: if the mayor asked me to speak at this time — it meant that there was a need for it. I therefore began to speak, saying whatever came into my head.

After I spoke, Gideon gave a brief speech, and he ended with the words: "Let there be light!" At once the neon streetlights lit up the entire area. In their light, everything seemed different, even the generation of the desert that had not yet rooted itself in the country.

When we rode back along lighted streets, we saw people who had come out of their houses to enjoy the lighted night. Around several of the street lamps circles of children and young people were dancing...

Kiryat-Gat is different from any other immigrant city that has been built in the heart of the desert. It is not like Dimona, which is surrounded by hills uninhabited for generations, nor like Kiryat Malachi, which has for a labour market the older settlements as far north as Gedera. The capital of Lachish is surrounded on all sides by the young villages of Lachish, as new as it is, and, like it, populated with new people, who have

"WHERE THE OUTPOST USED TO BE..."

only recently arrived, — and yet have already made the desert blossom and covered it with broad fields of cotton and peanuts and sugar-beets. The function of Kiryat-Gat is to serve the villages faithfully, to accept and process their produce, to manage the bargaining and trade, to seek better markets, to supply the cultural and social needs — to shine upon its surroundings and to be a city and mother in Israel.

XXVII

THE SIGNAL FIRES OF LACHISH

"And the king of Babylon's army fought against Jerusalem and against all the cities of Judah that were left, unto Lachish and unto Azekah, for of the cities of Judah there remained the fortified cities."
(Jeremiah, 34, 7)

"We have set watchmen for the signal fires of Lachish... For Azekah is no longer seen."
— from the Lachish letters

Lachish was the last fortified city to hold out after "all the cities of Judah that were left" had fallen, and the lights of Azekah were no longer seen. One after the other the signal fires went out, as the fortified cities surrendered to the sword of Sennacherib. Only the lights of Lachish still flickered from afar in the final nights of terror. They gladdened the heart of the besieged Jerusalem and strengthened the arms of its heroic defenders — until Lachish itself went up in flames...

Of the days of greatness of the ancient Lachish nothing is left but the ruins in the depths of the *tel*. The 'Lachish letters' were discovered there, and among them one from the commander of Jerusalem to the commander of Lachish: "We have set watchmen... for the signal fires of Lachish." These words have become the motto for the standard of the revived Lachish. The legendary Lachish has become a settled region, tied to the adjoining regions with ties of friendship and of rivalry. Of the "ancient" Lachish of five years ago nothing is left but the area on the eastern border, for the Lachish of today has spread west, north, and south.

When you reach Bet Guvrin and go into the chain of hills bordering the distant mountains of Hebron wrapped in blue secrecy, you find yourself in a landscape of stony hills barren for generations. From the ridge of the hills, you have a marvellous view: at the foot of the hills lies the entire region of Lachish; and on the other side, to the east — Hebron, city of the fathers — today, an enemy city.

The area on the border of Hebron was known for its hostility long before the War of Independence. In the riots that periodically swept the country, the Arab villagers from Duweimeh and Kubeiba in this area played a leading part in attacks on the Jewish settlements.

Through these hills passed an important road, linking Gaza and Hebron. For six years after the War of Independence this area was uninhabited, and the Jordanians recognised no border. From the borders of Hebron infiltrators struck deep into Israeli territory. Arabs ploughed and sowed fields that today belong to the *moshavim* of Lachish and Amatzia. Scouting units of the army kept up a constant struggle with these infiltrating *fellahin*. Night after night shots echoed in the mountains, and both sides suffered casualties. Gangs of *fedayin* lay in ambush in the mountains, concealed in caves and crevices in the cliffs.

In those years the area along the length of the Hebron border was nicknamed "the Israeli Texas", which is to say: Israel's "Wild West". Men from the border settlements rode armed over the wide grazing lands, like "cowboys". At that time it seemed very romantic. We said in jest that we ought to send them for the night all the tourists who complain that there is no "night life" in the country...

There are three border settlements: Nekhusha, Amatzia, and Lachish; each of them is of a different type of settlement, and each belongs to a different political movement: Nekhusha is a religious kibbutz; Lachish is a *moshav-ovdim* (of Tnuat Hamoshavim); and Amatzia is a *moshav-shitufi* (of Tnuat Cherut). But how should we below regard them with any partiality, when we raise our eyes to the hills and know that they are protecting us from the enemy and from danger? How could we care to which party or which movement they belong, these young people who enable us to walk through the fields of Lachish unarmed and without fear? The Arab refugees who abandoned Duweimeh know every path and every crevice in the mountains of Hebron and in the hills of Khulieqat, to the Gaza Strip. Before the settlement of these three border points there were continual clashes in the area. From here the infiltrators came to carry out their sabotage, stealing and smuggling. These few young people — guards of the borders — have blocked the breach with their bodies.

On the eve of Pesach 1956, the Nakhal group celebrated its first harvest "after two thousand years", and on the same day declared that Lachish was now an independent settlement, and no longer needed the assistance of the army.

We went to the celebration, despite the news that two days before there had been a battle with infiltrators on the Lachish road in broad daylight, and one of our soldiers had been killed. To our dismay, we saw that there was still no paved road connecting the border setlements with the rest of the region. When we rode through the fields of Lachish, we were entranced by the sight of a sea of grain spreading over an area of thousands of dunams. The stalks, almost as tall as a man, bent their yellow heads in the breeze. I recalled a similar scene in the fields of the Ukraine, the granary of all Russia.

The guests, most of whom were parents of the young settlers, were taken out to the fields in wagons and tractors, where they were seated on tables of straw arranged on the side of a hill. It was in the afternoon, and the rays of the setting sun flooded the gold of the wheat with all the colours of the rainbow. Surrounding us, on the ridges of hills, were young men and women with rifles, standing guard.

At the foot of the hill on which we were sitting a stage had been erected for the performance of a play set in ancient times. At the moment when the shepherd-king appeared, the settlement's flock of sheep poured over the hill and reached the stage together with the king. The landscape and the primitive glory of this scene were deeply affecting: however, most of the audience left at the end of the celebration, when darkness fell on the ominous mountains of Hebron. The young settlers continued with their celebration, singing and dancing: this was their home.

Have five years also passed on the eastern border of Lachish? Has the Lord enlarged our borders here as well?

In Nekhusha, which overlooks the border of Etzion, is a young Nakhal group. Almost none of its first founders remain; there are few married couples. It has fields which promise a good income, yet Nekhusha still has the appearance of a border outpost.

Moshav Lachish has changed its appearance. Houses have been built for the settlers, the best houses in the entire region. The 'moshavnik' feels a close tie to his home, and the young people who settled in Moshav Lachish checked every detail of the plans, and even added IL 1800 apiece of their own for improving the houses. Moshav Lachish arouses envy in the hearts of its neighbours, Amatzia and Nekhusha. It has 25 married couples, and an infant in almost every house: lofty, simple human happiness. But so far, only 25 of the 60 houses that were built are occupied. The rest are still vacant. The settlement corporation, "Amika", refused to turn over the houses to unmarried members.

I received contradictory reports about the progress of the *moshav*: a drought year, the yields were still low, transportation raised costs. But all these are passing troubles. There is an enormous reserve of fertile land, a plan for a vineyard of raisin grapes, and for an orange grove.

The main problem is a lack of members; there is no one to do the work. Twenty bachelors, left homeless after the married couples moved into their houses and the 'collective' broke up, left Lachish for a year and went to seek their fortune. They came down from the mountains of Hebron, in which they had invested more than four years of their lives — and what years! — because they were not "suited" for the conditions of the place. They did, indeed, work and watch and do their job, but an unmarried man cannot build up a farm if there is no collective framework.

The bachelors remained 'out of bounds' and they scattered throughout the country; their loss is badly felt in Moshav Lachish. Their searches have not yet brought about the desired results: few young women are eager to go live on the Jordan border. Several of them told me that they could find a partner if they would "gild" her. Apparently it is possible to "buy" a bride, as do our neighbors across the border — the only difference is that here the money is paid to the bride herself, rather than to her parents. The prospective bride wants her husband to furnish the house, buy a gas stove, an electric refrigerator and a washing machine, a radiogram and all the other household equipment; and some kind of transportation is also desirable. But without this "dowry" the bride won't budge.

I spent a Sabbath in Amatzia. Eleven kilometres of a bumpy dirt road winding between the hills that separate Amatzia from the main highway. The bus does not go into this settlement. The members jokingly say that Amatzia isn't to be found; you have to find it. The spot is nearer to Hebron than to Kiryat-Gat, and practically isolated from the rest of the country. At night one can see only the flickering lights from the huts of the Arabs in the villages of Jordan. And in the distance the lights of the hostile Hebron sparkle like an evil eye.

When the Lachish region held its fifth anniversary celebration, there was a meeting between representatives of the settlements and a committee of government representatives. Time was limited, and each of the representatives was allotted only a few minutes in which to present the requests of his village. When it was the turn of the secretary of Amatzia, a tall, thin young man named Meir, he spoke briefly in a monotonous, seemingly indifferent voice:

"We want to see 'Egged' (the national bus company). We've been in Amatzia for five years, and we still haven't seen a public bus in our settlement. We have to walk eleven kilometres to reach the highway. It's too far. We want electricity from the main power line, and not from a generator that breaks down every second day and leaves us completely cut off, without even a method of calling for help in case of an emergency. We want to drink water that comes from the 'Mekorot' pipeline, and not from pits of rainwater left by the Arabs who used to be in the area..."

After his speech, a member of the *moshav* Shalva, an immigrant from Tunisia, made a unique speech:

"I also have a request for my village, and in the name of my village I ought to make it, but after Amatzia, *I cannot*... When I heard the member from Amatzia speak, I recalled a story my mother used to tell me when I was a child and demanded things she could not give me. This is the story:

"'Once there was a poor man who had a large family, and he was unable to support them. When he came home tired and exhausted, his wife would nag him and the children would cry from hunger, until he could stand it no more, and decided to put an end to his life. The man climbed a high mountain nearby, in order to throw himself from the cliffs. When he reached the top of the mountain, he found a peapod there. He opened it, ate the peas, and threw the pod over the cliff. He leaned down to throw himself over the cliff, and at that moment he saw a man at the foot of the cliff who picked up the empty pod and ate it.

"'The man who had planned to commit suicide shuddered, and in his heart determined. I must not commit this sin: there are men who are even poorer than myself.'..."

Sunrise in Amatzia is a scene that makes life worth living. The landscape is magnificent. Here one can see ruins of ancient palaces, and in the destroyed Arab village are many pits for collecting rainwater and for storing grain.

Here, too, there are few settlers, and only a few married couples. The members of Amatzia have been living in huts for five years, for their houses are still unbuilt. I was surprised that not one of them complained, even of the drought, although they have many problems. The settlement is actually on the border, and there *is* no border in the usual sense of the word. There is only a white stone lying in a field to mark it, and the people of Amatzia plough up to the stone. The Arab across the border also ploughs up to the same stone...

The drought that has gone on for three years is wiping out the grazing lands of Amatzia, which are also being damaged by the Bedouin of the Negev and their herds, who have come north with the government's permission. Amatzia has 300 head of cattle. The settlers on the border conserve the grazing lands and use them in turn, but the Bedouin get there first, and destroy all the available grazing. Hundreds of shepherds with tens of thousands of sheep cover the fields. They leave behind them trodden fields and thousands of bales of scattered straw. The members of Amatzia tried to negotiate with the Bedouin, and even held a 'kumsitz' in their honour, but nothing helped. The member who told me about all this added:

"When we threaten them with arms, they cross the border — that is, the white stone — and they mock us from Jordan..."

"And why don't you put up a fence?"

"They'd steal the fence and take it to Jordan, too! Our government doesn't allow them to be in the area of the Lachish border. They have permission to graze their herds only in the area of Bet Guvrin. But the Bedouins play innocent and pretend they don't understand the orders."

In the late afternoon, the members gather in the clubroom, or go to a 'kumsitz' in the huts of one of the couples; the young housewives bake cakes and welcome guests, as they do everywhere in the world.

On Saturday night, the surprising report reached me that the "gang" had decided to travel into Kiryat-Gat and see a film. Had they lost their minds? — But thinking it over, there was really nothing so surprising about it, for not even a film reaches the Hebron border: there are so few people that it doesn't pay to show a film here. And so the desire is strong to get away from the settlement once in a while, and to see something new, to be among a crowd...

A lottery was held among the members to see who would go — the number of places in the pickup truck was limited. This time I too surprised the youngsters: I asked for a place in the car, for I wanted to go with them.

"I don't want to go to a movie," I said. "But I would like

to spend the night in Kiryat-Gat. Then I can reach home early in the morning."

The young men and women took their seats in the pickup truck with their rifles, as though they were back in the days of the Palmach, and went forth to the "operation" of going to a movie. The eleven kilometres separating Amatzia from the paved road leading to Bet-Guvrin seem ten times as far at night, for there are no lights of settlements twinkling in the distance. But when we reached the top of the hill at Shakhariya, a sea of lights suddenly appeared below us — the lights of Kiryat-Gat; that night they looked to me like the lights of Paris. From here we could see even the shopping centre of Kiryat Gat with its coloured neon lights. How beautiful the city is at night, when you come down to it from the border of Hebron!

Kiryat-Gat passed by, and the truck sped on. What had happened?

"Why spend the night in Kiryat-Gat?" the young men said to me. "We'll take you home. It's all right, we'll only miss the newsreel..."

Were these the same young men from the Palmach who had once brought me home from the deserted village of Masmiya?— No, of course not; but they were the same kind.